# The Happiness Fantasy

'With compelling clarity, wit, and wisdom, Carl Cederström cuts through the disabling illusions ceaselessly promoting the personal pursuit of happiness, offering instead an altogether richer, more compassionate, embrace of life and its vicissitudes.'

Lynne Segal, author of *Radical Happiness: Moments of Collective Joy*

'In this lively and acerbic book, Carl Cederström provides a compelling history of how a particular psychoanalytic ideal of happiness sucked us in, promising total fulfilment but ultimately trapping us in a lie.'

Will Davies, Goldsmiths, University of London

'A wonderful piece of work.'

Simon Critchley, New School for Social Research

'Happiness is big business – and big politics – these days. But as Cederström reveals in this sharp and engaging book, its recent history can be disturbing. Combining humour with a much-needed scepticism, he shows that in a world of happiness, not all is smiles.'

Darrin M. McMahon, author of *Happiness: A History*

'Pleasure was at the heart of the liberation struggles of the 1960s but has morphed into a new form of ideology and tyranny, fed by the capitalist logic of incessant consumption. The happy self is not only a fantasy, an imperative to fulfil our potential, but also the impulse behind a wide variety of economic enterprises, orgasmic workshops, drugs, therapies, etc. Cederström's *The Happiness Fantasy* is a well-written, lively, and critical study of the fantasy that has wormed inside the core of our culture.'

Eva Illouz, Hebrew University of Jerusalem

Carl Cederström

# The Happiness Fantasy

polity

First published in 2018 by Polity Press
Reprinted 2018 (three times)

Polity Press
65 Bridge Street
Cambridge CB2 1UR, UK

Polity Press
101 Station Landing
Suite 300
Medford, MA 02155, USA

ISBN-13: 978-1-5095-2380-1
ISBN-13: 978-1-5095-2381-8 (pb)


A catalogue record for this book is available from the British Library.

Library of Congress Cataloging-in-Publication Data
Names: Cederström, Carl, 1980- author.
Title: The happiness fantasy / Carl Cederström.
Description: Medford, MA : Polity Press, [2018] | Includes bibliographical references and index.
Identifiers: LCCN 2018004122 (print) | LCCN 2018006644 (ebook) | ISBN 9781509523849 (Epub) | ISBN 9781509523801 (hardback) | ISBN 9781509523818 (pbk.)
Subjects: LCSH: Happiness.
Classification: LCC BF575.H27 (ebook) | LCC BF575.H27 C43 2018 (print) | DDC 152.4/2--dc23
LC record available at https://lccn.loc.gov/2018004122

Typeset in 11.5 on 16 pt Minion Pro by
Servis Filmsetting Ltd, Stockport, Cheshire
Printed and bound in the UK by CPI Group (UK) Ltd, Croydon, CR0 4YY

For further information on Polity, visit our website: politybooks.com

# Contents

# Introduction

*Judge*: Just what is it that you want to do?
*Heavenly Blues*: Well, we wanna be free. We wanna be free to do
what we wanna do.

*The Wild Angels* (1966)

## The Happiness Fantasy – An Obituary

As an expression of what we desire and long for, the happiness fantasy is a shared fantasy of the good life. Like all fantasies, it brings together a set of moral values – functioning as a kind of road-map to the happy life. The nature of these fantasies changes over time and space. For the ancient Greeks, the ultimate happiness fantasy was a still and quiet life of contemplation. To get there was not easy. You had to rise above yourself, break out of the ordinary condition of being human, and cultivate a long list of virtuous faculties.

The happiness fantasy that will concern me in these pages is the fantasy that has dominated the rich West for almost a century. It is a fantasy of self-actualization, according to which there is only one way to become happy, and that is by reaching your full potential as a human being. It is to live in a spirit of authenticity, where you are called upon to live *your* life, as opposed to someone else's life. It is to pursue happiness in the form of pleasure, whereby the most rudimentary daily activities become moments of potential joy. And it is to submit yourself to the market, working hard to develop your brand and gain a competitive edge.

In short, it is a fantasy of realizing your true inner potential, both as a market resource and as a human being. This happiness fantasy emerged as an idea in the 1920s, reached its peak in the 1960s, and came to a definite end in the early hours of 9 November 2016.

Just before 3 a.m., in the Hilton Ballroom on Manhattan in New York City, Donald Trump slowly came down the stairs from the side of the stage to the soundtrack of Air Force One, giving a double-thumbs up, before addressing the cheering audience:

'Working together, we will begin the urgent task of rebuilding our nation and renewing the American Dream. I've spent my entire life in business, looking at the untapped potential in projects and in people.'

On my way to the university that morning I kept hearing those two words ringing in my head: *untapped potential.* They had been on my mind for a while. I had talked about the human potential movement in my previous lecture, showing clips from seminar trainings in the 1960s with people screaming and shouting as a technique for stripping away layers of their inauthentic selves to reach their true potential.

These scenes were taken from the Esalen Institute in California, which opened in 1962. Throughout the Sixties, Esalen was the go-to place for people who wished to explore their inner beings. Psychedelic drugs and Eastern mysticism were combined with modern psychology to test new routes to expand and extend the human self. The theme for the first season was 'human potentiality', an idea that had come to one of the organizers after attending a talk by Aldous Huxley a couple of years earlier in which he extolled the need to recognize the fact that that all people are different, and to find ways to actualize all people's potentialities.[1]

In contrast to Huxley, Trump has never been interested in human differences. His women look the same, as do his men. He does not share the anti-authoritarian ethos of the human potential movement, but talks and acts like an autocrat. In the year that has passed since he took office, Trump has tried to impose a travelling ban targeting people from mostly Muslim countries to enter the United States, cracked down on LGBT rights, and outspokenly supported white supremacists.

In my reading, the idea of human potentiality reflects not just a version of the American Dream but also a vision of happiness, a vision that has spread across the Western world over the last century, optimistically suggesting that everyone can take control over their lives and actualize their inner potential. I argue that this is a kind of fantasy, as I put it in the title of this book. But when I say fantasy, I am not suggesting that this version of happiness is unreal. On the contrary, it is a fantasy that is very real insofar as it has mobilized people's emotions and, by extension, the way they envision the good life.

The subject of this book is the happiness fantasy that became widely popular in the Sixties countercultures. It was a dream of a different world, pitted against a society based on conservative values, wealth accumulation, domination, and violence. Half a century down the line, this fantasy has taken on an entirely different form. It is no longer posed as an alternative to capitalism, but an integrated part of it. It is no longer standing in opposition to domination; it is part of domination.

'We really didn't see it coming, the new world of rabid individualism and the sanctity of profit,' Jenny Diski wrote in her book *The Sixties*.[2] The Sixties was a time of 'striving for individuality and a nagging urge to rebel against the dead middle of the twentieth century'.[3] And then, without Diski and her friends seeing it, came Margaret Thatcher and Ronald Reagan and stole their favourite words – liberty, permission, freedom – and twisted their meaning so they would fit their right-wing political agenda.

They were yet to realize exactly *how* different the sense of those words now was. Hearing Trump talk about human potentiality that morning, more than fifty years after this notion was first expressed by Huxley, I couldn't help thinking that this fantasy was now officially dead and buried.

In that sense, this book is an obituary.

## Happiness – A Moral Fantasy

When we talk about happiness, we seem to be talking about fantasies, more specifically moralistic fantasies, which set out a template for the good life. This claim may appear strange when applied to conceptual statements about what happiness is or isn't. But it makes more sense when we look at happiness historically. It then becomes clear that whatever we consider to be a happy life today, in the rich West, is something altogether different from what it was thought to be in the past.

In his book *Happiness: A History*, the historian Darrin M. McMahon provides an account of how the notion was expressed and embraced over time, going back to the birth of Western civilization, as many such accounts do, in ancient Greece.[4]

For Aristotle, one of the first to pay significant attention to the topic, happiness consisted of being a good person. The happy life, what the Greeks called *eudaemonia*, was one lived ethically, guided by reason and dedicated to cultivating one's virtues. Soon after, the Epicureans would connect happiness to pleasure. They argued that a good life should be devoted to whatever brought pleasure. They were no hedonists, though, and preached a strict regulation of desire. To be happy, Epicurus himself said, he needed no more than a barley cake and some water.

The Stoics gave no elevated status to pleasure, arguing that a person had the capacity to be happy no matter how daunting and painful the circumstances of life might be. Much later, Christianity, as preached and practised throughout the Middle Ages, shunned pleasure altogether and regarded pain as the more useful path to, if not a happy life, then a sort of divine union in the afterlife. That desired state could not be attained in life on earth, but only as a gift from God, in heaven.

The Renaissance, though, brought happiness from heaven back to earth. It was not until the Enlightenment that it became a right – something that each and every person was able to pursue and attain. When Thomas Jefferson wrote in the Declaration of Independence that the pursuit of happiness was an unalienable right, he did not just intend to say that man should pursue pleasure, but that he should also have the right to acquire and possess property.

What we esteem today, in the rich West, has its own distinct flavour.

Contrary to the message of Christianity, according to which we abandon ourselves to achieve divine union, we are now asked to pursue union with ourselves. To be happy in a time when we prize authenticity and narcissism, we need to express our true inner self, get in touch with our deeper feelings, and follow the path set by ourselves.

We are also far from the ascetic Epicureans. In today's hedonistic consumer culture, we are impelled to desire more than barley cake and water. To be happy, we should optimize our enjoyment, whether through food, partying, relaxation, or sex.

And unlike the work-shy Greeks of antiquity, we are assumed to find happiness through work and by being productive. We are required to curate our market value, manage ourselves as corporations, and live according to an entrepreneurial ethos. When no sin is greater than being unemployed and no vice more despised than laziness, happiness comes only to those who work hard, have the right attitude, and struggle for self-improvement.

These are some of the moral values that seem to undergird happiness today: be real, enjoy yourself, be productive – and most important, don't rely on other people to achieve these goals, because your fate is, of course, in your own hands.

This is a popular message, and has been for some time. It is drummed into the unemployed and poor, who are led to believe that their misfortunes are symptoms of their inferior attitudes and inability to take ownership over their lives. They are reminded that they are not working hard enough.

### Whatever Happened to the Promise of the Sixties?

These moral values have had a profound influence on Western culture since the twentieth century. They have shaped the way we think about happiness – and therefore also how we lead our lives. When self-actualization appeared as a desirable notion in the 1950s and 1960s, it was easy to understand its appeal. Gone were the gloomy days of Freudian unhappiness. At last, people were not obliged to conform to someone else's imposition of an idea of how they should live. Stability and boredom could be traded for mobility and adventure, as expressed in the film *The Wild Angels* from 1966 when the rebellious biker

Heavenly Blues (played by Peter Fonda) is asked by a judge what it is that he and his gang of bikers want to do, and he responds: 'Well, we wanna be free. We wanna be free to do what we wanna do.' Then he adds, talking on behalf of his cheering biker friends in the background: 'And we wanna get loaded. And we wanna have a good time. That's what we're gonna do. We're gonna have a party.'

The kind of life that had previously been shunned as immoral became largely acceptable in the 1960s, although still regarded with suspicion among some conservatives, as was the case with the snooty American reporter who famously ridiculed John Lennon and his wife Yoko Ono when they spent two weeks in a hotel bed in 1969 protesting against the Vietnam war. Scornfully responding to Lennon's claim of being everyone's spokesman, the reporter sneered, 'Whatever race you're the representative of, I ain't part of it.'

The dream of peace and happiness, as staged by Lennon and Ono in their bed-in, remains an evocative image of the Sixties revolution, a period that fused the twin pursuit of authenticity and sexuality into a common refrain of the good and peaceful life.

But over the course of the last half-century, this happiness fantasy has become all the more difficult to sustain. The dream of pursuing the life one wants, as opposed to a life that is predetermined either by one's parents or by one's community, has always been closely related to the dream of mobility. Granted, setting out on a path towards a more authentic life is very difficult if one is unable to leave behind the inauthentic life one currently leads. Today, however, few have the financial resources to move, whether socially or geographically. According to a report from 2015, three-quarters of all Americans believed the American Dream was on the wane, which is not very surprising given that as many as one-third of the American people lived in poverty for at least two months between 2009 and 2011. In the face of poverty, stability appears to be more important than mobility, as a 2015 Pew survey revealed, suggesting that 92 per cent of all Americans now prefer stability over mobility.

A similar transformation can be noted in relation to hedonism. Devoting oneself to enjoyment was perhaps a daunting pursuit in the first part of the twentieth century, when thrift and frugality were morally endorsed. But in the kind of consumer society we experience today, the pursuit of pleasure is the cultural norm. Already in 1976, the American sociologist Daniel Bell noted that hedonism – the notion of pleasure as a way of life – was both the cultural and moral justification of capitalism.[5] But this does not mean we are suddenly living a more enjoyable life. As the social theorist Mark Fisher has suggested, the problem today is not our inability to gain pleasure, but our 'inability to do anything else *except* pursue pleasure'.[6]

There are also good reasons to question the ingrained belief that work is the path to self-actualization, especially now, in the context of precarious labour, where many people are unable to know when and from where their next pay cheque will appear. Trying to make the office a happier place is not in itself problematic, if that implies carefully listening to the needs of the employees. Nor is it wrong for people to want meaningful jobs, as long as they can make a living off those jobs. And it isn't necessarily a bad thing to dissolve the line between work and life, provided one is fortunate enough to do what one wants, as was the case with John Lennon, who refused to regard music as work. But what we experience today, as happiness at work has become compulsory, is something else entirely. When greeting customers, service workers are compelled to smile in an authentic manner. Or else they might lose their jobs, as was the fate for one employee at the UK fast-food chain Pret a Manger.[7] In an era of 'Do What You Love', graduates should be grateful for getting the chance to intern for an exciting company with a cool brand name and should therefore accept long hours of pointless work with no pay. More often than not, blurring the boundary between work and life means answering emails long after the working day is over, rather than greater 'self-actualization'.

We know that the levels of social mobility remain stunningly low in both the United States and the United Kingdom. And yet the delusional notion that all people, irrespective of background and circumstances, are able to transform their lives through the power of positive thinking continues to be a strong conviction, promoted by a range of influential politicians, including Donald Trump.

## A Cruel and Menacing Doctrine

The happiness fantasy that blossomed in the United States in the 1960s, based on the optimistic notion that everyone could actualize their inner potential, has now turned into a cruel and menacing doctrine, strategically employed to sustain and normalize the structural inequalities in contemporary capitalism. This is not to say that everything was rosy in the 'Age of Aquarius'. Reading Joan Didion's essay 'Slouching Towards Bethlehem' should put any such myths to sleep. When she goes to San Francisco in the late spring of 1967, she does not find 'brave hopes' and 'national promise', but a place in disarray, with adolescents drifting from city to city, families disappearing, and a mother giving her five-year-old daughter peyote and acid.[8] A similarly dark portrayal of the hippie era is found in a recent television documentary about the Danish commune Christiania, telling the story from the viewpoint of the children, who were left to their own devices, while their parents were preoccupied with their spiritual (drug-infused) awakening. I don't want to romanticize the Sixties by claiming that the fantasy and the reality were perfectly compatible. What interests me here is the transformation of this happiness fantasy. How can we explain why the notions of individual freedom and sexual liberation that flourished in the Sixties, as a protest against paternalistic institutions and capitalist exploitation, have undergone such a dramatic transformation? Whether or not these values were diluted in the first place, they have now become re-packaged as corporate slogans, used as a rhetorical technique to enlist subjects in their own exploitation.

To illustrate what has become of this fantasy, we have to go no further than to Donald Trump. If someone like John Lennon symbolized the dreamlike character of this happiness fantasy in the 1960s, as someone who was authentic, sexually liberated, and immensely productive in his creative work, Donald Trump personifies the nightmarish quality it carries today. Although different to Lennon in all significant respects, Trump nevertheless embodies these same qualities. He is authentic, in the sense of setting his own path without paying too much attention to what others say or think. He is a product of hedonism, making no attempts at concealing his love for young models and fatty fast food. And he is a self-acclaimed workaholic, boasting about sleeping no more than four hours a night.

## A Brief History of the Happiness Fantasy

Even though this happiness fantasy reached its apogee in the 1960s, the story goes further back than that. It begins with the Austrian psychoanalyst Wilhelm Reich and his unconventional interpretation of sexual drives, which made a strong impression on Freud when they first met in Vienna in the early 1920s.[9] Soon Reich was introduced as the youngest member to Freud's inner circle. But only a few years later, as Reich's theories and practices had taken a more eccentric and sexual turn, he became widely unpopular with his fellow analysts, was pushed to the fringes of the community, and eventually, after a few more years of controversy, was expelled both from the local Viennese and Berlin psychoanalytic societies and from the International Psychoanalytic Association. What makes Reich interesting to this story is that he offered an unusual yet distinct vision of happiness in which he combined the moralistic imperative of being authentic with that of sexual pleasure. It was a fantasy of happiness, beyond sexual repression. More specifically, it was an outspokenly moralistic fantasy, because what determined whether or not you were healthy, Reich argued, was your ability to reach what he called full orgasm. Failing to do so was an indication that you were ill.

Reich was not the first to link happiness to authenticity. We could think of a range of precursors, from Rousseau via the Jena romantics to the American transcendentalists, such as Ralph Waldo Emerson and Henry David Thoreau. Neither was Reich the first to link happiness with sexual pleasure. For one, Marquis de Sade claimed that sexuality and pleasure constituted the foundations for happiness and individual freedom. But even so, Reich was the first to bring these two ideals together and express them in the form of a happiness fantasy, or what he liked to call 'sexual happiness'.

A few years after his death, Reich's ideas became central to the growing set of Californian bohemians, and the countercultural movements that were beginning to take form. By the end of the 1960s, Reich's name and ideas were evoked when young people from both sides of the Atlantic revolted against what they saw as oppressive state apparatuses. And when self-transformation training centres started to emerge in the 1960s, they were often based on Reich's ideas.

Over the next few decades, these centres became a growing mass phenomenon that would attract hundreds of thousands of people across the United States and elsewhere.

The happiness fantasy that was sold in these places, and that people hoped to gain access to, was the fantasy of sexual and existential liberation, as Reich had expressed it a few decades earlier.

The crucial moment in this story, I claim, is in the mid-1970s, at which point many of these training centres began to develop a more commercial approach. People would go to these places and subject themselves to a range of experimental techniques, similar to those offered in the beginning of the 1960s, but now with the hope of becoming a better and more successful professional. At around this time, the human potential movement, with its original focus on self-transformation, assumed a more commercial nature. Self-actualization was not just an end in itself; it was also an effective means to become materially richer and professionally more successful – in short, a strategy to become better attuned to the market. In the 1980s and 1990s, as corporations began developing strong corporate cultures, they turned to the human potential movement for inspiration. As they realized that this was an unprecedented opportunity to make employees more committed to work, large corporations started to integrate catchphrases about human potentiality into their corporate cultures, and, in some cases, even used these expressions when formulating their mission statements.

The question that concerns me in this book is how this particular happiness fantasy, as it was originally devised as a protest against society, became co-opted and integrated into corporate cultures, mainstream psychotherapy, and pharmaceutical discourse. How can we explain why the notions of self-actualization and self-development, which appeared at a time defined by affluence and abundance, are still endorsed today, in a time defined by precarity and austerity? And finally, as this happiness fantasy no longer has any meaningful role to play, what are the alternatives?

These are the questions I wish to address in the course of this book. I begin with Wilhelm Reich, the radical psycho-analyst whose ideas came to have a profound influence on the Sixties and the revolt against tradition and conservative values, especially with regard to sexual and personal liber-ation. My claim is that our present-day happiness fantasy, which to a large degree organizes our notion of the good life, emerged in the work of Reich. I will then consider the peculiar afterlife of these ideas, as they were picked up by business-minded self-help gurus and turned into mass training programmes in which people learnt how to combine personal liberation with financial success. This era came to be known as the 'Me Decade', during which self-ishness and narcissism were hailed as moral values. I will argue that the culture of narcissism that prevailed in the 1970s is dramatically different from the narcissistic culture we have today insofar as young people are now obliged to engage in forms of self-promotion. They are narcissists not by choice, but necessity. We will then take a closer look at corporations and how they adapted themselves in the 1970s to a new culture in which authenticity and pleasure were esteemed. Words such as freedom and empowerment, which had been levelled against corporations in the 1960s, began to seep into management discourse during this period, employed to attract consumers and workers alike.

The ambition was to eradicate the line between production and consumption, on the one hand, and the pursuit of happiness, on the other. From this moment, the happiness fantasy was not in opposition to work, or to capitalism at large, but something that was pursued through work. A similar transformation is at play when we consider the use of drugs. From being integral to the happiness fantasy of the Sixties, as a way of enlarging the world and exploring new dimensions of the mind, drugs have today become a means by which we can adapt ourselves to the demands of society. With support from psychiatry and pharmaceutical companies, they help us achieve normality and become functional, productive, and streamlined. Groups of Silicon Valley entrepreneurs experiment with ayahuasca and LSD to become more creative. Large parts of American college students ingest Adderall and Modafinil to enhance their productivity. But not all drugs are easily compatible with the happiness fantasy. Considering the ongoing opioid crisis, it is hard to see a connection between drugs, on the one hand, and creativity, productivity, and happiness, on the other.

In the following chapter, I will consider hedonism and the injunction to enjoy, which is inseparable from the moral foundation of consumer capitalism. From its roots in Epicureanism, hedonism has come to signify the right to pleasure, whether in the form of consumption or sex. This model of a right to pleasure, which exploded in the Sixties, came to its logical endpoint when Trump was caught on tape saying that, as a celebrity, you have the right to do anything – 'grab them by the pussy'.

My claim in this book is that the happiness fantasy, which has shaped our notion of the good life for the last century, has lost its appeal. It no longer serves the purpose of the many but only that of the few. It is no longer about enlarging human possibilities, but about narrowing them. And it is by no means a feminist dream, but a male-oriented fantasy of self-mastery.

I will end this book on a relatively optimistic note, claiming that we need to reimagine the happiness fantasy. Instead of thinking about happiness in individualistic and delusional terms, we need to think about it as a collective struggle and a commitment to truth. I believe something like this is already happening. As I write this, a revolution is taking place, with courageous women coming together en masse to reveal their experiences of sexual abuse. By doing so, they expose the structural violence at play, which by no means is restricted to figures such as Harvey Weinstein and Donald Trump, but includes many other men who, by virtue of their positions, have been permitted to do what they want to do, in the name of a 'right to pleasure'. This is a story of pain and sorrow. But to witness the crumbling of the power structures that have protected these men is also invigorating, and perhaps the start of something new. Maybe we can now begin to articulate new fantasies of what we consider to be the good life, fantasies that could lead us away from the dead-end of our contemporary culture, based on the cult of authentic individuality, relentless competition, and the imperative to enjoy.

This is not a book about happiness as such. It is a book about the history of an idea. Or the history of a fantasy – a fantasy that emerged in the work of Reich in the 1920s, reached its peak in the revolutionary zeitgeist of the Sixties, became absorbed into consumer culture and conservative politics in the 1980s, and died recently, when Trump came into office, unknowingly referring in his acceptance speech to Huxley and his vision of a world of human potentiality and a deep respect for human differences – a vision that was diametrically opposed to what is now proposed by Trump and his administration.

# 1

## In Bed with Wilhelm Reich

I know how bitterly you resist your integrity, what mortal fear comes over you when called upon to follow your own, authentic nature. I want you to stop being subhuman and become 'yourself.' 'Yourself,' I say. Not the newspaper you read, not your vicious neighbor's opinion, but 'yourself.'

Wilhelm Reich, *Listen, Little Man!*[1]

### Encountering Reich

I first came across the ill-fated psychoanalyst Wilhelm Reich (1897–1957) in Adam Curtis's documentary *The Century of the Self*. Or so I thought. I watched it a few years ago, watched it again, then started using clips from the film in my own teaching, to illustrate the dramatic change of American culture in the 1960s. It contains wonderfully evocative scenes of people screaming and shouting in dimly lit seminar rooms with soft mattresses. In these encounter sessions, participants were instructed to peel off the inauthentic layers of themselves. The belief was that, by acting out their true inner selves, they would become free. Even though Reich died in 1957, a few years before the human potential movement would take off, he played an important role in its making. He was an important precursor, a spiritual inspiration. Like these movements, Reich was more optimistic about humans' inner potentials than he was about the organization of society, which, in his view, played an oppressive role, preventing individuals from becoming who they really were. Reich's story, as it was told in the documentary, was brief but nonetheless riveting. From a hailed analyst in Vienna in the 1920s to a permanent outlaw, kicked out not just of the psycho-analytic establishment in the 1930s but also from several countries (mostly Scandinavian ones), and then, as an old and slightly mad man, imprisoned in the United States for promoting and selling his home-produced orgone accumu-lator, a life-sized wooden box with metal interior, designed to enhance a person's orgastic abilities. The box was later parodied and immortalized as the Orgasmatron in Woody Allen's *Sleepers*.

But it would turn out that it was not in Curtis's docu-mentary that I had first encountered Reich. I had known him rather intimately for more than a decade, through the music of Kate Bush, and her wonderful tune 'Cloudbusting', which appeared on her 1985 album *Hounds of Love*. When I recently watched the music video, I realized the song was all about Reich, chronicling his tragic fate. The video opens with two Sisyphus-like figures, played by Donald Sutherland (as Reich) and Kate Bush (as Reich's son), pushing a huge covered object up a hill. Once they reach the top, exhausted and happy, they uncover a metal construction with wheels and handspikes, looking like a massive anti-aircraft gun. As Reich aims the gun at the sky, his son looks in awe at him. By the end of his life, Reich grew delusional, and believed his so-called 'orgone gun' was useful not just to alter the weather, and produce rain, but also to defend earth from an imminent threat from outer space. He died in prison at the age of sixty.

More than a madman, Reich came to have a profound influence on how we think of happiness today. I'm not suggesting that he discovered an entirely new notion of happiness, which then went on to become the dominant template for Western culture. He was, however, the first to bring authenticity and sexual pleasure into a coherent notion of happiness. As such, he played a crucial role in forming the kind of happiness fantasies that now, about a century later, have become neatly integrated into our culture.

What makes Reich interesting for the present analysis is not just his theories, as they were expressed in his writings, often with anger. I would agree with Philip Rieff when he says that reading Reich 'is like going to a pacifist meeting: one is a little frightened to witness so much aggression displayed by men pleading an end to aggression'.[2] Reich's texts, especially the later ones, are hyperbolic and aggressive, as when he writes: 'I want you to stop being subhuman and become "yourself",' repeating, '"Yourself," I say' (see epigraph above). These texts are not, I must admit, particularly pleasant to read. Neither can I find any visible signs of genius, as so many others have claimed to have seen. But that does not make Reich any less interesting. What makes him fascinating is his unflinching ability to always be in the right place at the right time, and inscribe himself in critical historical moments. Or the wrong place at the wrong time, depending on one's point of view. Because the fact remains that he was there, first in Vienna, when Freud and his colleagues lay the foundations for what would go on to become a massively influential view of the human psyche. He was working in one of the free clinics in Vienna when psychoanalysis was made available for the first time to common people. And Reich was there again, albeit as a shadow, when large parts of the American youth took to the streets (or fields) to rebel against the old bourgeois world of conformity, and set out what became known as the sexual revolution. The fact that Reich became conservative in his final years, and voted Republican, was just one among many other ironies, which seemed to be the defining feature of his life.

After his death, Reich came to embody a particular fantasy, a fantasy about happiness beyond repression. As the age of conformity came to an end in the early 1960s and the individual was no longer compelled to shoulder and act out predestined roles, Reich became the kind of cult figure that many searched for. His books were widely read among a new generation of young American bohemians from the 1940s onwards. He became a convenient symbol, hailed by countercultural figures such as William Burroughs, Fritz Perls, and Paul Goodman. In a time defined by social upheaval, political experimentation, and existential confusion, Reich became a potent symbol for hope and transformation.

Young women did not want to be like their mothers, whose image was tied to the well-ordered and infinitely sad housewife. And young men certainly didn't want to follow in their father's footsteps, taking up a mind-numbing job in a big corporation, coming home late in the evening to eat tasteless food in front of the television – and then keep on doing that, day in day out, until they would finally drop dead from a heart attack.

In Jack Kerouac's 1958 semi-fictional novel *The Dharma Bums*, the character Japhy Rider (based on the poet Gary Snyder) envisions a revolution against this kind of monotonous life. In his revelation, he saw all forms of peculiar characters coming together, from rucksack wanderers and young Americans to Dharma Bums and Zen Lunatics. They all

refused to subscribe to the general demand that they consume production and therefore have to work for the privilege of consuming, all that crap they didn't really want anyway such as refrigerators, TV sets, cars, at least new fancy cars, certain hair oils and deodorants and general junk you finally always see a week later in the garbage anyway, all of them imprisoned in a system of work, produce, consume, work, produce, consume.[3]

It was in this cultural climate that Reich's ideas gained traction. He launched a theory of happiness which, in the decades following his death, would become neatly integrated into our culture. Thinking about happiness as a pursuit of authenticity, aiming to bring about a life of pleasure, is by no means controversial today. It is the standard notion. Happiness is an individual pursuit – a choice.

But that is not how happiness was viewed back then. When, as an analyst in Austria in the 1920s, Reich started to promote his own vision of happiness, based on the assumption that the individual had to be sexually liberated, he met fierce resistance. He would later describe these struggles in a short and angry book called *Listen, Little Man!*, written in 1945. 'For twenty-five years I've been speaking and writing in defense of your right to happiness in this world, condemning your inability to take what is your due,' he wrote. According to Reich, we are our own masters, and are free to do what we want to do with our lives. 'No one is to blame for your slavery but yourself. *No one else*, I say.'[4] At the time of writing these words, conformity and security were still the prevailing cultural norms. A happy life was immediately associated with material comfort, psychological security, and a stable family life. As the historian Jackson Lears notes, 'advice from *Good Housekeeping* and similar magazines was "Don't be afraid to conform", or to encourage your children to. The family became the factory turning out "well-adjusted" adults.'[5]

It was also in the domestic safety of family life that one was supposed to find happiness. This was one of Alexis de Tocqueville's findings from his travels in America in the 1830s. In *Democracy in America*, Tocqueville notes:

When the American retires from the turmoil of public life to the bosom of his family, he finds in it the image of order and of peace. There his pleasures are simple and natural, his joys are innocent and calm; and as he finds that an orderly life is the surest path to happiness, he accustoms himself without difficulty to moderate his opinions as well as his tastes.[6]

Reich, however, considered the family as a 'factory for authoritarian ideologies'[7] and saw the emotional bond between family members as a disease, calling it familitis. Security and comfort were not gateways to happiness. They were its barriers. 'You plead for happiness in life, but security means more to you, even if it costs you your backbone or wrecks your whole life.'[8]

In addition to being addicted to the comforts of domestic life, these people were also willing slaves to consumer capitalism. Too scared to pursue the authentic life of individual freedom and sexual happiness, they wasted their lives watching mindless television shows or being brainwashed by radio commercials. 'You listen to commercials on the radio, advertisements for laxatives, toothpaste, shoe polish, deodorants, and so on.'[9] According to Reich, these people were not worthy of happiness, because, to be happy, you need to *will* happiness. 'Now do you understand why happiness runs away from you. *Happiness wants to be worked for and earned.* But you merely want to consume happiness. It runs away because it doesn't want to be consumed by you.'[10]

Today, more than half a century later, we will find Reich's words echoed in any number of life-style magazines and self-help books, and even in politics and business. Freud's pessimistic vision of human happiness, meanwhile, is entirely out of fashion. While Freud is arguably still the more respected of the two, it seems that Reich got the last word, at least when it comes to shaping our present culture of happiness. Freud and Reich embody two conflicting visions of happiness, so conflicting, we will see, that it led the two men to permanently stop talking to each other.[11]

## When Reich Met Freud

In the summer of 1918, a few months before the end of World War I, Wilhelm Reich, then twenty-one, arrived in Vienna. He was a strikingly pretty boy, with dark penetrating eyes, but the war had left him penniless and he owned no other clothes than his shabby military uniform. In his autobiography, *Passion of Youth*, Reich described how he lived, for two whole years, on oatmeal and dried fruit. One diary entry dryly reads: 'Sitting in my room wearing gloves and fur coat, studying chemistry.'[12]

After a brief stint studying law, which he found 'dull and remote',[13] Reich switched to medicine, finding it only marginally more stimulating. The curriculum made no mention of sexology, an omission that Reich and some of his fellow students found unacceptable.

Despite being a traditional and bourgeois place with a penchant for sentimentality, Vienna was also a centre for new provocative ideas, whether in philosophy, art, or music. It was in an attempt to connect with these currents

– and especially the study of sex and libido – that Reich and his fellow students had set up a seminar group. More than a year passed before they had mustered courage enough to seek advice from Sigmund Freud.

'I had come there in a state of trepidation,' Reich later described, 'and left with a feeling of pleasure and friendliness.'[14] Freud had proved to be a caring and willing mentor and helpfully furnished the young men with a selection of his own books. For Reich, it became the start of a fourteen-year-long intellectual relation; but one which would end in 'bitter disappointment'.[15]

What started as an intense intellectual collaboration, with Freud referring to Reich as one of his most talented adepts, ended, in the early 1930s, in a bitter fight over politics and the structure of the family. At the heart of this conflict, I argue, we find two conflicting visions of happiness. Reich believed strongly in a revolutionary politics that would materialize itself only when people had become sexually liberated. And to achieve such liberation, he argued, we must first dismantle the family. It constrains the freedom of its members and prevents them from being happy. Children are forced to obey. As a result, they become miserable and docile. Which was the case with the masses. As he wrote in *The Function of the Orgasm*: 'The structuring of the masses of people to be blindly obedient to authority is brought about not by natural paternal love, but by the authoritarian family. The suppression of the sexuality of small children and adolescents is the chief means of producing this obedience.'[16] Throughout Reich's work we find a romantic notion of what he interchangeably calls 'natural happiness' and 'sexual happiness'. He saw this as the polar opposite to suppression, obedience, and authoritarianism. Freud, meanwhile, was more sceptical about this form of happiness. While he agreed with Reich that sexual repression was indeed a problem of their time, he did not see sexual liberation as a natural route to happiness. In one of his later works, *Civilization and Its Discontents*, Freud suggests that, even though we are all pursuing happiness, we are not destined to find it.[17]

Many years later, not long before his death, Reich offered an interview in which he spoke out about his relation to Freud. 'Would you look at this picture of Freud,' Reich asked the interviewer: 'I don't know whether you will see what's in that picture. I didn't see it when I received it from him in 1925. Can you see what's in the picture?'

The interviewer went over to the picture, looked at it, and answered, hesitatingly, that, well, there may be something there. 'It's a very sad expression,' Reich commented, 'true despair.'[18]

According to Reich, Freud was a hopeful and potent man when they first met. But then, in the mid-1920s, all of that changed: he developed cancer and lost his zeal. 'Now cancer in my research,' Reich continued, 'is a disease following emotional resignation.'[19]

Reich implied that the reason Freud developed cancer was because he wasn't sexually satisfied. 'I don't think his life was happy,' Reich explained. 'He lived a very calm, quiet, decent family life ... but there is little doubt that he was very much dissatisfied genitally.'[20]

Here, in these words, we find the uncensored expression

of Reich's moralistic happiness fantasy. Happiness was synonymous with the ability to find sexual satisfaction. It implied reaching a state of perfect harmony, in which one could form a complete union with oneself. Failing to be genitally satisfied was an indication of illness, which was expressed in the form of perversion, resignation, or, as in the case of Freud, fatal cancer. We can see how, in articulating this fantasy of happiness, Reich draws on a beatific fantasy of the good (sexual liberation, authenticity, potency, etc.), which is pitted against a horrifying fantasy of the corrupt (perversion, cancer, resignation, etc.). As we will see, Reich did not confine this happiness fantasy to the domain of the individual. When he became more political in the latter part of the 1920s, it came to inform his entire vision of society – a vision that would later be shared by many others.

## The Making of a Sexual Revolutionary

Reich's life was in many ways different from Freud's. His story starts in 1897, four decades after Freud's birth, in a small farm in the Austro-Hungarian Empire, in today's Ukraine. In his autobiography, *Passion of Youth*, Reich describes a somewhat odd household, plagued by sexual intrigues. At the age of four he eavesdropped on the house-maid when she was having sex with the coachman. Reich later described this experience as producing in him 'erotic sensations of enormous intensity'. The year after, at the age of five, Reich began masturbating his younger brother's nursemaid. 'I climbed on top of her,' Reich describes, 'lifted her dress, and reached feverishly for her genitals (to her apparent enjoyment).'[21] A few years later, at the age of eleven, he lost his virginity to the family chef. And during most of his childhood, he pleasured the family's horse with a riding crop.[22]

At the age of ten, Reich found out his mother was having an affair with his private teacher. He used to dwell outside the door, listening as they made love, and entertained the thought of storming the room and blackmailing his mother, saying he would let his father know unless she agreed to have sex with him.

But he never got to that point, because his father found out anyway. Afraid of his retaliation, his mother tried to commit suicide by downing a bottle of detergent. She was saved by her husband, but after two more attempts, she finally managed to take her own life. Reich was then thirteen years old.

A few unhappy years later, Reich's father died too. At the age of seventeen, Reich was taking over the responsibility for a large farm and his younger brother.

This might seem like a suitable upbringing for a person who would later become synonymous with the sexual revolution. Sure, one should always be careful not to conflate a person's life with their work. But perhaps it is possible to view this the other way around. As Susan Sontag wrote in her introduction to Walter Benjamin's *One Way Street*: 'One cannot use the life to interpret the work. But one can use the work to interpret the life.'[23]

Either way, it was with this upbringing, and a few years

of war in the front line, that Reich arrived in Vienna in 1918 to start his studies at the university. The following year, after having become acquainted with Freud, he was given the opportunity for the first time to present his own psychoanalytic research. It was a small but exclusive group of analysts who had come to listen to the young Reich. Notably nervous, Reich presented a paper about Peer Gynt in which he argued that Gynt suffered from narcissism and delusions of grandeur, caused by libidinal conflicts. The analysis made a great impression on the audience, and Reich was taken up as the youngest member in Freud's inner circle, the Vienna Psychoanalytic Society.[24] What they did not know at the time was that Reich strongly identified with Peer Gynt and that he, too, had bouts of narcissistic delusions of grandeur.[25] It did not take very long, though, before they found out.

Reich's early fascination for sex had not waned. When he started his practice, he was given unprecedented opportunities to explore these issues, not just in theory, but also in reality. As a student, his success with women had been limited. He felt out of place in the local dancehalls, and reproached the women who rejected him. But when he became a prominent analyst, things changed. Not only did he acquire a new sense of status, he was also provided with a new kind of space, which no doubt suited him better than the dancehalls.[26] During analysis, he received the undivided attention that he had long desired.

So it was not surprising that it was through analysis that he would meet his first wife. Colleagues objected with outrage, of course. Sleeping with your patients was – and is

– one of the greatest taboos in the trade. But Reich defended his actions. He had not slept with her *during* the analysis, he claimed, but only *after* it was completed, at which point she had finally become her own true self.[27] In the midst of the protests, Freud defended his young disciple.

During the first few years of the 1920s, Reich showed no interest in politics. He was under financial strain and had to work long hours tutoring students to get by. But in the mid-1920s, as his circumstances grew better, his political interest came to life. He joined the German youth movement, Wandervogels, where he met socialists, pacifists, and sexual libertarians. Inspired by the anarchist Gustav Landauer, these young freedom lovers revolted against all forms of authority. They looked with disdain on their parents' bourgeois life-style and sought freedom in the mountains, which became the natural destination for their excursions.[28]

With his appointment at the newly opened clinic known as the Ambulatorium, which was located a stone's throw from Vienna's general hospital, Reich could combine his growing interest in politics with psychoanalysis. Up until this point, psychoanalysis had been a practice available to a select few. It was expensive. Few could afford it. But when the free clinic opened, psychoanalysis was made available to everyone. The only requirement was a willingness to disclose one's secrets. This site was a perfect fit for Reich. In the course of his employment at the Ambulatorium, he met more than seventy people. They came from all sorts of backgrounds. He treated industrial workers, office workers, students, and farmers.

Reich exploited this opportunity. Curious to learn more about people's sexual life, he began to collect their stories. In 1924, as he became the head of one section, he gained access to the other analysts' files, and the following year he published his first book, *The Impulsive Character*, based on the stories he collected at the Ambulatorium. Reich was particularly interested in what he called impulsive characters – patients who, in his words, 'have an extra something which the simple neurotics lack'. He was keen to understand the motives of those with self-castrating tendencies, such as 'the impulsive-driven female patient who can masturbate to orgasm only if she bleeds profusely from the vagina, and who severely injures her cervix with a knife handle and winds up with a dropped uterus'.[29]

What defines the impulsive character, Reich claimed, was their unhealthy sexual nature, brought about by an inadequate sexual education. As these characters grow up, they lack the ability to relate to their sexuality. 'Neither masturbation nor intercourse,' Reich wrote, 'can afford relief, for the whole libidinal organization is torn apart by disappointment and guilt feelings.'[30]

Based on the rich material that Reich had collected, he thought he had found the key to why so many people suffered from neurosis. In short, the problem was to do with their inability to reach full orgasm. A few years later, with the publication of *Functions of the Orgasm*, he summarizes his findings: 'Of the hundreds of cases which I observed and treated in the course of several years of extensive and intensive work, there was not a single woman who did not have a vaginal orgastic disturbance. Roughly 60 to 70 percent of the male patients had gross genital disturbances.'[31]

Convinced he had solved the fundamental problem of psychoanalysis, Reich became all the more radical in his analyses. One woman who was living in a sexless relationship was asked by Reich to initiate a sexual relation with a younger man.[32] The very yardstick for a successful therapy became the patient's ability to have an orgasm. Reich called this orgastic potency. He likened the human to an onion, and the role of the analyst was to help patients peel off the layers and break through their character armour. Hidden beneath these layers was an essentially good and loving creature, Reich believed. And the aim of analysis was to break free from this character armour. As Reich writes:

> This characterological armoring is the basis of isolation, indigence, craving for authority, fear of responsibility, mystic longing, sexual misery, and neurotically impotent rebelliousness, as well as pathological tolerance. Man has alienated himself from, and has grown hostile toward, life. This alienation is not of a biological but of a socio-economic origin. It is not found in the stages of human history prior to the development of patriarchy.[33]

Reich wrote in a time defined by scientific curiosity and experimentalism. Yet, as he began to refer almost all forms of psychological suffering to the inability to reach full orgasm, fellow analysts in the Vienna circle became ill at ease. In the mid-1920s, Reich was still regarded as one of the most important analysts of the country. But around this time, as his views grew more radical, the critics grew in number. One of Freud's adepts, Richard Sterba, accused Reich of being a genital narcissist. Another influential analyst, Paul Federm, labelled him aggressive and paranoid. Other colleagues simply called him the orgasm fanatic.[34]

## Renunciation or Total Orgasm

Freud's essay 'The Future of an Illusion' from 1927 can be read as a direct response to Reich's romantic vision of the human as an inherently good being. In Freud's pessimistic essay, the individual is described as a destructive being with anti-social and anti-cultural tendencies.[35] For these reasons, a civilization has to be based on 'coercion and renunciation of instincts'.[36] Freud did not just object to Reich's vision of people's inherent virtue; he also championed his own version of authoritarianism, claiming that without some degree of imposed repression, the masses would go berserk. 'For masses are lazy and unintelligent … and have no love for instinctual renunciation, and they are not to be convinced by argument of its inevitability.'[37] In an elitist tone, Freud continues: 'It is just as impossible to do without control of the mass by a minority as it is to dispense with coercion in the work of civilization.'[38]

When Freud wrote these words in 1927, his relation to Reich had already begun to deteriorate. Meanwhile, Reich's political engagement grew stronger. He read Marx and found his work to be as radical for the economy as Freud's work had been to psychiatry. Soon after, he read Engels,

Trotsky, and Lenin and had a political awakening joining the medical wing of the Austrian Communist Party in
1927. From now on, his task was to combine Marxism with
psychoanalysis.

For Reich, the masses were beautiful and potentially
liberating. They were not defined by laziness or unintel-
ligence, as Freud had suggested. The masses only became
dangerous when they were repressed. If they could learn
how to reach full orgasm, and as a result live happily and
authentically, they would naturally come together in an
organic and friendly manner. Together they would form
what Reich envisioned as a genital utopia.

Freud, however, did not believe in the overcoming of
humanity[39] – especially not by overthrowing the old
repressive order and replacing it with a new, sexual utopia.
For him, such thoughts were delusional and a testimony
that Reich had misunderstood the fundamental insights
of psychoanalysis, namely that the individual has inherent
aggressive tendencies and, as an unconscious being, 'is not
even master in its own house'.[40] For those reasons, there
could be no utopian society based on sexual liberation.

Their disagreement on this point was insurmountable.
Reich thought that unhappiness was imposed externally,
through authoritarianism and paternalism. Freud, on
the other hand, saw it as an inevitable condition of being
human. They met a last time in 1930, at Freud's lakeside
villa. Reich later recalled, 'Freud couldn't follow me. It
was not the character-analytic technique, it was the sexual
revolution that bothered him.'[41] I would argue that what
bothered Freud was Reich's vision of collective happiness,

which he viewed as the logical conclusion of a genital revolution. This was Reich's happiness fantasy.

Reading the short and often polite correspondence between Reich and Freud, spanning from 1924 to 1939, reveals little about their disagreement over the concept of happiness. A better place to look is Freud's *Civilization and Its Discontents*. In a letter to his friend Lou Andreas-Salomé, Freud referred to the book as an 'inquiry concerning happiness'.[42] In fact, Freud was first planning to call his book *Unhappiness in Civilization* (*Das Unglück in der Kultur*). But he later replaced 'unglück' with the more suggestive 'unbehagen', which was more difficult to translate. Freud himself suggested *Man's Discomfort in Civilization*,[43] but his translator Joan Riviere decided against that.

Reich later claimed that the entire book was written as a response to him. More specifically, it was conceived as a reaction against a paper that he had presented in Freud's home in 1928, entitled 'The Prophylaxis of the Neuroses'.[44] The paper didn't go down well with Freud and his colleagues from the Vienna circle. Reich later recalled the 'cold atmosphere' from the meeting in Freud's home. The discussions became caustic and Freud struggled to retain his temper. It was clear to everyone at this point – including Reich himself – that Freud regarded him as awkward, and increasingly difficult to deal with. As Reich later remarked, 'I was the one who was "unbehaglich in der Kultur".'[45]

The purpose and intention of people's life, Freud writes at the outset of *Civilization and Its Discontents*, is happiness. People strive to be happy, and wish to remain so.[46] To this end, people resort to the 'programme of the pleasure principle', which seeks to maximize pleasure and minimize pain. But there is a problem with this pursuit:

> One is inclined to say that the intention that man should be 'happy' is not included in the plan of 'Creation'. What we call happiness in the strictest sense comes from the (preferably sudden) satisfaction of needs which have been dammed up to a high degree, and it is from its nature only possible as an episodic phenomenon.[47]

Here, we can see clearly the difference between Freud and Reich. The nature of happiness, according to Freud, is episodic and arises when our dammed-up needs are satisfied. For Reich, in contrast, happiness is a lasting state in which our needs are constantly satisfied. In such a state, the individual would achieve autonomy and sexual independence. Sexuality had to be free and natural, completely liberated from internal and external restrictions. And the only way to become a satisfied and happy person was by first achieving genital satisfaction.

According to Freud, there are at least two problems with this assertion. First, the pleasure principle cannot be prolonged indefinitely. After a while, 'it only produces a feeling of mild contentment', because 'we are so made that we can derive intense enjoyment only from a contrast and very little from a state of things'.[48] When the contrast disappears, so too does enjoyment. Second, pursuing enjoyment without renunciation is doomed to backfire: 'An unrestricted satisfaction of every need presents itself as the most enticing method of conducting one's life, but it means putting enjoyment before action, and soon brings its own punishment.'[49] Following the pleasure principle, then, will not lead to lasting happiness. Either it will result in a mild contentment, which grows weaker and duller over time, to the point at which all sensory pleasure eventually fades away altogether. Or it will produce its own dissatisfaction, which will be at least as painful as the satisfaction was pleasurable.

In choosing between these two strategies, people may be better off trying to steer clear from unhappiness and dissatisfaction. That way, they avoid the intensity of enjoyment-induced suffering. While happiness is in short supply, unhappiness isn't. It is everywhere. It comes from the superior power of nature, which, at any given time, can wipe us away. It comes from our own bodies, which rarely operate as we want, and will eventually break down. And it emerges from the relations we have with other people, whether with family, state, or society.

Unhappiness comes easily and naturally to us, Freud claimed. But this is something we don't want to confront. Instead we blame our unhappiness on external causes, such as the oppressive nature of civilization. We want to convince ourselves that 'civilization is largely responsible for our misery, and that we should be much happier if we gave it up and returned to primitive conditions'.[50] To hold on to this fantasy, we blame civilization for having stolen our pleasure. Rules and restrictions have disconnected us from what we most want and enjoy. To Freud, this was only a fantasy aiming to obfuscate the painful awareness that, as humans, we will never be perfectly attuned to what we desire.

Needless to say, Reich did not like what Freud had to say in *Civilization and Its Discontents*. It was standing in direct opposition to almost everything he believed about human happiness, sexual satisfaction, and the vision of a society beyond renunciation. For Reich, *Civilization and Its Discontents* was an expression of Freud's resignation and cancer.

Even though happiness was not a central concept in Freud's work until the publication of *Civilization and Its Discontents*, we can find it in a few other places in his writing, including one of his earliest works, *Studies in Hysteria*, published in 1895, at which point Freud was in his late thirties. By the very end of the book, Freud explains that one of the key tasks of the analyst is to help patients better arm themselves against unhappiness. When patients had asked him in what way they can be helped through analysis, Freud famously responded that 'much will be gained if we succeed in transforming your hysterical misery into common unhappiness'.[51] It seems, then, that Freud did not alter his view on happiness as a consequence of his physical suffering, as Reich claimed, but remained suspicious of happiness throughout his career. As Philip Rieff remarked, 'Freud embarked on a modest experiment: his doctrine promises not more happiness but less misery.'[52]

### Decline and Fall

At the time when *Civilization and Its Discontents* was published, Reich had broken with his family and moved to

Berlin, where he had joined the Communist Party. Berlin had offered him a new start, and a new audience, which seemed much more receptive than that in Austria. But the visit was stopped short. As Hitler seized power in 1933, Reich feared for his life and fled back to Austria. Soon after he left, his work was publicly burnt together with that of other Jewish authors, including Freud.

The following six years, from 1933 to the outbreak of the war in 1939, Reich spent in Scandinavia. He first arrived in Denmark, where he self-published *Fascism and Mass Psychology*, a book-length attempt to blend Marxist theory with psychoanalysis. He returned, again, to the question of the masses. Unlike Freud, Reich thought that the masses were not inherently dangerous. People only became aggressive once they were disconnected from their own true nature and made afraid of their own sexuality. 'The man reared under and bound by authority has no knowledge of the natural law of self-regulation,' Reich writes. '[H]e has no confidence in himself. He is afraid of his sexuality because he never learned to live it naturally. Thus, he declines all responsibility for his acts and decisions, and he demands direction and guidance.'[53] Fascism thrived when people suffered from poor self-esteem. 'Fascist mentality is the mentality of the "little man", who is enslaved and craves authority and is at the same time rebellious.'[54]

Reich had moved to Denmark to work as a teacher. At first, he seemed to have gained the influence he desired, but this was short-lived. When one of his followers ran for the Danish Riksdag based on his sex-political agenda, he became known as a controversial figure whose ideas would corrupt the youth.[55] The reception of *Fascism and Mass Psychology* was largely hostile. In one particularly savage review, published in the Danish communist newspaper, the book was called counterrevolutionary. As a consequence, Reich was expelled from the Danish Communist Party.[56] His visa was not renewed.

After a short spell in Sweden, a place he intensely disliked, Reich moved to Norway, where he stayed until 1939. There he developed a new type of therapy, where patients were asked to take their clothes off and lie down on their back, legs in the air, and breathe heavily. Reich gave the patients a massage in an attempt to make them relaxed and receptive to reach full orgasm. The method was first called orgasmotherapy, but later changed to character-analytic vegetotherapy.[57] Reich believed that this kind of therapy had an emancipatory goal: to bring freedom both to the individual and to society. 'Here was a therapy that would change the world – but only by changing the self,' as Rieff put it in *The Triumph of the Therapeutic*. 'In Reich, these strands of socialism turn around a curious messianic belief in therapy, forming a doctrine of salvation.'[58] Later, many patients, including Reich's own son, would complain that the therapy had inflicted serious bodily harm on them.

Reich had now been kicked out of Germany, Denmark, and Sweden, as well as the Communist Party and the International Psychoanalytic Association. Disillusioned, he withdrew from the public scene and immersed himself deeply in his own scientific experiments. He wanted to observe what he called vegetative currents. His experiments were unconventional. For example, he mixed various food items in a pot, then studied them with his microscope.[59] Despite these eccentric methods, or perhaps because of them, his experiments were eventually successful. Or so he believed. In 1939 he claimed to have observed what he thought was one of the greatest scientific discoveries to that date. He had seen a form of radiation, a type of cosmic energy, which he called orgone energy. This energy would be a cure-all medicine, potent enough to combat any disease, including cancer.

In 1938, as fascism reached Norway, Reich made a short interruption in his scientific work, and fled to the United States. He settled in a two-storey brick house in Forest Hills in Queens, New York, where he resumed his experiments. Having discovered that orgone energy was airbound, he began devising boxes in which this energy could be captured and intensified. The result was the orgone accumulator – a wooden box clothed with metal, large enough for a human to step into. Reich was convinced that the box would heighten a person's orgastic potency. In 1942, he bought an estate in Maine, which he named Orgonon. For the next six years, he continued his experiments in peace.

But this would all change when Mildred Edie Brady published a savage article in *The New Republic* in 1947. In the article, Reich was described as 'a heavy-set, ruddy, brownhaired man of 50, wearing a long white coat and sitting at a huge desk'. In a sardonic tone, Brady profiled him as a fraudulent analyst spouting paranoid fabrications about society.

Between periods of training students in his theories and putting patients into orgone accumulators, he will tell you how
unutterably rotten is the underlying character of the average
individual walking the streets, and how, in the room across
the hall where he works on his patients, he peels back their
presentable surfaces to expose the corrupted 'second layer' of
human personality.

The author went on to mock Reich's theories, and then
added that the 'growing Reich cult' could not be entirely
blamed on the psychoanalytic establishment, but that it
should indeed take some responsibility. Whereas 'druggists,
plumbers and even hair dressers have to have a license to
practice their skills', she wrote, 'anyone can call himself a
psychoanalyst, hang out a shingle and take patients'.[60]

The article in *The New Republic* had devastating conse-
quences for Reich. Soon after it was published, a letter was
sent to the Food and Drug Administration (FDA), alerting
them that Reich 'appears to be supplying his patients with
a gadget which will capture the seemingly fantastic substance "orgone" and accumulate it for the benefit of the
person who occupies the space within this device'.[61] The
FDA opened an investigation and travelled unannounced
to see Reich at his estate in Maine. When finding out that
250 orgone accumulators had been constructed at the site
and shipped off to customers, the administration reported
'that we have here a fraud of the first magnitude being per-
petrated by a very able individual fortified to a considerable
degree by men of science'.[62] The FDA also suspected Reich
of leading a sexual racket of some sort.

The FDA issued an injunction against the accumulator, which was later violated. As a result, Reich was sentenced to two years in prison, and all of his accumulators and literature were to be destroyed. One month later, under the supervision of the FBI, all of Reich's accumulators were chopped up with axes and his books (251 in total) burnt. Reich died the following year in prison.

### Legacy: Involuntary Leader of the Sexual Revolution

But Reich was soon resurrected. As students flocked to the streets in the late 1960s, he was turned into a countercultural superstar. He was no longer a lunatic, but a natural leader to a new set of anti-authoritarians who wished to overthrow authority. In Berlin, protesters hurled copies of Reich's *The Mass Psychology of Fascism*. In Frankfurt, protesters were advised to 'Read Reich and act accordingly'. And in Paris, Reichian slogans, such as 'Total Orgasm', were graffitied on the walls of the Sorbonne.

Reich's popularity among the bohemian left had begun much earlier. Already from the late 1940s, he had had cult status among the anti-authoritarian youth, especially the new bohemians who had started to occupy California. In a 1947 article for *Harper's*, Mildred Edie Brady described these newcomers as a 'different crowd', with 'beards and sandaled feet', wearing 'corduroys and dark shirts'. These young bohemians lived in 'uncarpeted rooms', with 'abstract paintings against rude board walls, canned milk and pumpernickel on a rough table, ceramic ashtrays and opened books on a packing box'. Their favourite word was 'affective', along with 'fecund', 'orgastic', 'magical', 'fluid', and 'natural'. They blended anarchism and psychoanalysis to form their own philosophy – 'holding on the one hand that you must abandon the church, the state, and the family', and then, on the other, 'offering sex as the source of individual salvation in a collective world that is going to hell'.[63] For this generation, who revolted against bourgeois morality, Freud was completely passé. Jung was a more appealing alternative, no doubt. But the ultimate hero was Reich. According to Brady, Reich's *Function of the Orgasm* was 'probably the most widely read and frequently quoted contemporary writing in this group'.[64] Following Reich meant that you could combine politics with sex, although for most of these people anarchism was mostly a convenient excuse to have sex. The principal belief for the young bohemians was a version of Reich's thesis:

> that if everybody else were only as healthy as you, instead of suffering from the psychic plague as most of them are, there would be no need for artificial compulsions, legal prohibitions, or for any of the oppressive machinery of the state. Everybody would be wholesomely self-regulatory. All would respond to 'the natural biological law' freely and spontaneously. In other words, through widespread orgastic potency, through a gonadal revolution, we would achieve the philosophical anarchist's ideal world.[65]

When Brady's article was published in the late 1940s, the young bohemians in California were still small in number, and their influence was limited. But that would soon change. In the next couple of decades, as the American counterculture exploded, California would become its main stage. In a prophetic essay from 1957, Norman Mailer claimed that 'the empty hypocrisies of mass conformity' were coming to an end. 'A time of violence, new hysteria, confusion and rebellion,' he argued, 'will then be likely to replace the time of conformity.'[66] Mailer claimed that, in the wake of World War II, with millions of people killed in the concentration camps, it had been impossible to 'maintain the courage to be an individual'. The post-war years were years of conventionality and depression, which had made the American people 'suffer from a collective failure of nerve'.[67] But all of this, Mailer thought, was about to change. To reinvent themselves, Americans were devising their own version of existentialism, spearheaded by the hipster, or what he also called the 'white negro'. For the hipster, it was imperative to live authentically, and as a consequence one had 'to divorce oneself from society, to exist without roots, to set out on that uncharted journey into the rebellious imperatives of the self'.[68]

One of the most important antecedents of this generation, Mailer claimed, was Wilhelm Reich. Reich's eccentric methods of analysis and his orgone accumulators posed a distinct alternative to the conventions of psychoanalysis, particularly the kind of analysis that aimed at making patients more functional, and, by extension, conformist. The risk with this type of analysis, Mailer thought, was that it tranquillized the patient, and wore him down. The patient was made 'less bad, less good, less bright, less willful, less destructive, less creative'. At the end of the analysis, the patient would be able to 'conform to that contradictory and unbearable society which first created his neurosis'.[69] Instead of changing the patient into a new, invigorated individual, analysis made him numb, sedated, and tired. It helped him 'conform to what he loathes because he no longer has the passion to feel loathing so intensely'.[70]

The aim of Reich's theories and practices was to make people thrive by liberating them from the chains of conformity. Reich's therapy, which enabled one to reach full orgasm, was perfectly suited for the hipster who, in Mailer's words, knows 'at the seed of his being that good orgasm opens his possibilities and bad orgasm imprisons him'.[71]

Apart from Reich, the other intellectual antecedent of this generation was the author Henry Miller. Miller, whose sexually explicit books had been banned in America, was one of the first iconic bohemians to settle in California. Shortly after returning from his ten-year exile in Europe, Miller had found and immediately fallen in love with the picturesque area of Big Sur, which he had first seen a few years earlier, when driving along the coast from Los Angeles to Monterey.[72] With Miller as a permanent resident, Big Sur developed a reputation among the new set of bohemians. In the words of historian Jeffrey J. Kripal, Miller would 'establish a legendary literary presence in Big Sur that would stamp the place as a mecca of sex, banned literature, and political anarchy'.[73] In 1957, after having lived in the area for more than a decade, Miller published a book about Big Sur, declaring his undivided love for the place. The explicitly sexual content that had featured in his earlier novels was now gone, replaced by what Kripal calls a 'panerotic nature mysticism'.[74]

As Miller's friends joined him in Big Sur, the place became known, in some circles, as a rural 'West Greenwich Village'.[75] And in 1962, as the two Stanford graduates Michael Murphy and Richard Price opened up the premises of the Esalen Institute, the region became a hot spot for freedom-peddling Americans. The first seminar was organized by Alan Watts, whose experimental work was an unorthodox fusion of Western psychology and Asian Tantra.[76] During the spring of 1962, Price and Murphy began organizing more seminars, and in the summer of that year, as they were putting together the programme for the autumn, they decided, as I noted in the introduction, that the theme should be human potentiality, a concept that Price had picked up from a lecture that Aldous Huxley had delivered two years earlier at the University of California, San Francisco Medical Center.[77] In that lecture, which was titled 'Human Potentialities', Huxley had claimed that humans have within themselves vast spiritual and intellectual resources that are never properly put to use.

The seminars offered at Esalen during that autumn included discussions on parapsychology, mind-opening drugs, the occult, behaviourism, art, and religion. The place became a melting pot for new experimental ideas, blending the philosophy and psychology of Mesmer, Swedenborg, Jung, and Freud with traditional Christian religion and Eastern mysticism. When pressed to define itself, Murphy and Price called it 'an alternative educational center devoted to the exploration of the human potential'.

Over the course of the next decade, an array of prominent people arrived at the institute, including Carl Rogers,
Abraham Maslow, Alan Watts, Aldous Huxley, and Gerald
Heard. They would later be known as the human potential movement, a phrase that was coined by John Leonard,
editor of *Look* magazine, in 1965.[78]

But no person would come to define Esalen in the way
that Fritz Perls did. Perls had been in analysis with Reich
for three years in Berlin during the 1930s.[79] Later, Perls
absorbed Reich's ideas about orgasm and politics and, in
his own words, 'made a kind of phallic religion out of it'.[80]

In 1964, Perls took up a permanent residency at Esalen.
He was in his seventies and well known for his pioneering
work in Gestalt therapy. On his arrival, he 'wore shirts and
sport jackets', which he soon swapped 'for brightly colored
jumpsuits'. He 'grew his beard and hair long so that he
resembled a dissolute Santa Claus'. His wife Laura Perls
described him as 'half prophet, half bum'.[81]

What makes Perls interesting for our discussion is not
only his connection to Reich, but also how his therapy illus-
trated the fantasy of liberating the self from all constraints
as a way to become healed.

At Esalen, he gave a weekend course in Gestalt therapy
for $46 per person. According to the 1964 brochure: 'Dr
Perls will explain the concept underlying Gestalt Therapy,
and will demonstrate some of the methods he has developed
for extending awareness and healing destructive divisions
of the self. These methods include the use of dialogue
(between therapist and patient and between aspects of the
self).' In practice, this meant that a volunteer sat next to

Perls. This was called sitting 'on the hot seat'. The aim was to break through the person's defence mechanisms. They were asked to describe their dreams, then act out different characters from the dream. The result was an emotionally charged one-person psychodrama. They were encouraged to cry and scream, and by the end of the session they were expected to kiss Perl's forehead.[82]

Even though Perls did not think much of philosophy – he liked to think of it as 'mind-fucking' or 'elephant shit'[83] – his seminar training had its own distinct philosophical underpinning. He wanted to make people understand that life was one long theatre act, and that they were all actors. It was only by acknowledging this truth that they could take ownership over their own lives. As Kripal explains, it was 'all about individuals becoming aware of their own play scripts, refusing to live in someone else's script, and taking full responsibility for their own chosen performances'.[84]

Like Reich, Perls wanted to break through the inauthentic layers of people's personhood that supposedly concealed the true nature of their beings. Bringing out this hidden self, Perls wanted to make his clients 'whole' and more 'authentic'. He referred to his technique as akin to brainwashing, by which he meant, not indoctrination, but 'washing the brain of all the mental muck we are carrying with us'.[85] Each workshop started with participants reading the Gestalt prayer, repeating lines such as 'I am not in this world to live up to your expectations,' and 'You are you, and I am I.'

Over the 1960s and 1970s, thousands of people flocked to self-development centres across the United

States in the hope of discovering their inner selves. At the heart of many of these training centres was Reich's notion of sexual liberation. What had been regarded as fraudulent and obnoxious ideas about the human self only a decade earlier had now become integrated into a new version of the American Dream and its quest for self-realization.

But Reich's ideas were visible not only in shouting crowds of students, countercultural hippies, and LSD-mongering anti-authoritarians. They were also integrated into mainstream psychology. During the 1930s, therapy was occupied with finding ways of 'adjusting' people to normality. As noted by the historian Jackson Lears, psychoanalysts now started to work for 'the betterment of the patient's total adjustment to life rather than the removal of a particular symptom'.[86]

A particular branch of psychoanalysis, known as ego psychology, had adopted Reich's method of analysing patients' defences. By adapting psychology to the core values of American culture, this branch became the dominant therapeutic practice in the 1950s.[87] It had devised a post-Freudian conception of the self, based on the assumption that there was a conflict-free zone within the ego. The role of therapy was to locate this zone and help the individual develop a strong and autonomous ego. In promoting this new version of therapy, analysts were able to offer more than 'common unhappiness'.

But as authenticity and sexual liberation became the new objectives among many Americans, even this 'happy-fied' version of Freudian analysis was struggling to attract people. It was too expensive, required too much time, and did not offer enough concrete results. Meanwhile, new humanistic therapies emerged in the United States. In contrast to Freudian analysis, they were better attuned to the spirits of the time, and their practitioners, such as Carl Rogers and Abraham Maslow, were better equipped to cater for people's more urgent needs. In *One Nation Under Therapy*, the philosopher Christina Hoff Sommers and the psychiatrist Sally Satel described these 'humanist' psychologists as a response against Freudianism and its relentless focus on human psychopathology.[88] These therapists were more optimistic in relation to happiness than were Freudians, claiming that therapy had the ability to bring about self-fulfilment. Better still, it didn't have to be expensive or take very long. As the sociologist Eva Illouz notes, this movement aimed 'to help one's own authentic self, whether that self needed to be unearthed or fashioned from scratch'.[89]

Only a decade after Reich's death in the late 1950s, his ideas had become integrated both in the new therapeutic movements and among self-exploring bohemians in California. The happiness fantasy, based on the pursuit of authentic selfhood and sexual pleasure, was no longer considered the ideas of a madman. Those ideas had gone mainstream. But this was only the start. As we will see in the next chapter, this particular notion of what it meant to live a happy and fulfilled life would go on to influence all sorts of domains, resulting not only in new ways of work, but also in new ways of relating to the self, ushering in what I will call a compulsory narcissism.

2

# Compulsory Narcissism

How should a person be? I sometimes wonder about it, and I
can't help answering like this: a celebrity.

Sheila Heti, *How Should a Person Be*[1]

## The Me Decade

In 1976, Tom Wolfe published a long essay in *New York*
magazine called 'The "Me" Decade and the Third Great
Awakening'.[2] On the cover of the magazine, we see
twenty-nine mostly white men and women standing closely
together in yellow T-shirts with the word 'Me' written over
their chests. They all face the camera and point their index
fingers at themselves, as if they had just scored a last-minute
goal in the World Cup Final.

The word 'narcissism' stems, of course, from Greek
mythology and the story of the young beautiful Narcissus,
who, after rejecting the nymph Echo, is cursed by the god

Nemesis to fall in love with his own mirror image, which he finds in the reflection of a pond. He remains stooped over his mirror image until he understands his love will remain unanswered and kills himself. The legend of Narcissus has since been retold many times, but it was not until 1898 that the sexologist Havelock Ellis coined the term 'narcissism' and related it to a state of 'absorbed contemplation and sometimes-erotic self-admiration'.[3] In his essay 'On Narcissism: An Introduction' from 1914, Freud assumed a primary narcissism to be present among all children,[4] and a necessary phase in the child's sexual development.

In the 1970s, narcissism became a concern also for those outside of psychoanalysis, especially for American journalists and social critics, who were looking for a word to describe what they perceived as a growing culture of selfishness, a culture that seemed to have emerged out of the disillusionment of the Sixties, and which celebrated the ideals of self-fulfilment and authenticity.

This generation of Americans were described as ordinary working men and women who had benefited from the economic growth in the preceding couple of decades. They entertained material and psychological comfort, what Philip Rieff called a 'plenitude of option'.[5]

As they transitioned from scarcity to abundance, these people could think of no better way of spending their time and money than on themselves and their pursuit to discover and actualize their inner selves. According to Wolfe, it all started with the Esalen Institute, which he described as a place that people went to in order to get a 'lube job for the personality'.

The happiness fantasy, which had been espoused by radical groups of the Sixties, had now reached the middle classes. Reich's notion of authentic selfhood and sexual liberation were no longer connected to socialism or a desire to overthrow society. They were pursued to achieve personal happiness.

Better still, self-actualization was now the path towards great incomes and new business opportunities. Participants of the new awareness courses learnt how to acquire and enjoy what lawfully belonged to them. The original message of human potentiality, as developed by Huxley, had now morphed into a cult of selfishness. This transformation was spearheaded by cunning salespeople and motivational leaders who, in their vision of human potentiality, blended the pursuit of happiness and self-actualization with a drive towards professional success and great riches.

The opening scene from Wolfe's essay was taken from one of these places, a programme called Erhard Seminar Training (or 'est', written in lower-case characters), where hundreds of people were lying on the floor in a hotel ballroom. Each of the participants shouted out what they most wanted to eliminate from their lives. Some of them wanted to eliminate their husbands and wives. Others their homosexuality and self-hatred. Others still hoped to get rid of their impotence or alcoholism.

Between 1971 and 1984, 700,000 people came to est to learn how to accept complete responsibility for their own actions and circumstances. When the participants were done, and had 'gotten it', they understood that there were no victims in the world.

## The Making of Werner Erhard

In 1953, the eighteen-year-old John Paul Rosenberg got married. Six years later, now the father of four children, he fled his home in Philadelphia. He took a new name, Werner Erhard, and moved to San Francisco, where he started selling encyclopaedias. In the mid-1960s, California had become a vibrant place for spiritual adventures, drug-infused experimentation, and personal freedom. Since it opened in 1962, Esalen had grown exponentially. From offering only four courses in the first year, it held more than twenty courses in 1965. At its peak, in 1968, there were as many as 129 courses.[6]

As a shrewd salesman, Erhard understood that this was an untapped market, waiting to be exploited. In his unflattering portrait of Erhard, *Outrageous Betrayal: The Dark Journey of Werner Erhard from est to Exile*, Steven Pressman writes: 'Werner Erhard, living in the grueling world of door-to-door sales, was quick to recognize the potential of a symbiotic connection between the practice of commercialism and the free-flowing idea from the human potential movement that seemed to be exploding all around San Francisco.'[7]

While Erhard had never attended the workshops at Esalen himself, he had greatly enjoyed Alan Watts's radio show about Zen. As noted above, Alan Watts was one of the first, and also the most popular, gurus at Esalen. He blended Eastern mysticism with the use of hallucinogenics and a longing for personal freedom. Another important influence was Fritz Perls and his Gestalt therapy. When later developing his own confrontational methods, seeking to break down the armour of the participants, Erhard would borrow heavily from Perls's methods, especially the infamous 'hot seat'.

Apart from Watts and Perls, Erhard was strongly inspired by the classic self-help literature from the 1930s, such as Napoleon Hill's blockbuster manifesto *Think and Grow Rich* and Dale Carnegie's *How to Win Friends and Influence People*.[8] In these books, Erhard had found an attractive image of the strong-willed individual and his wondrous abilities to move mountains, change circumstances, and close important business deals. Yet another influence was Scientology. In the latter half of 1968, Erhard enrolled himself in its introductory communication courses. He continued his engagement with the Scientologists for a couple of years, albeit half-heartedly. In December 1970, as he was supposed to take a more active part in marketing their courses, he suddenly dropped out. Instead he joined a pyramid-sales company called Holiday Magic, which, as part of their rich menu of products and services, also offered an intense motivation training called Mind Dynamics. Erhard had been a participant in the training himself, and then went on to become an instructor. In January 1971, after having obtained the San Francisco franchise, Erhard filled a Holiday Inn hotel with thirty-two students for his first official training session.[9] He was remarkably successful. Much more so than his fellow instructors, who had been struggling to attract even thirty people to their classes. Erhard, however, went on to attract as many as a hundred people.[10]

Confident he would be better off on his own, Erhard announced that he was leaving Mind Dynamics to open up his own, independent business. He called it Erhard Seminar Training, but preferred to only use the abbreviation est, because est, in Latin, means 'it is', and Erhard thought that the word 'is', in all its simplicity, reflected rather well the key insights of the training. On the last day of the intense four-day programme, the trainees were expected to have fully absorbed the message that, as Erhard put it, 'What is, is, and what ain't, ain't.'[11]

est became an instant success, and word of the new training programme spread rapidly.

Erhard's training certainly drew on the mystical and spiritual language of his forerunners at Esalen. But he added a pragmatic element. Attending a seminar would not just be a useful experience for soul and mind. It also had to achieve something more tangible. This is also what seemed to appeal to so many people: that the programmes were intensive and practical in nature, promising to make people more efficient and successful.

The training typically took place in large hotel ballrooms. The participants, who had paid $250 each, would meet for two intensive days on a weekend, and then resume again the following weekend, for two additional days, to finalize their training. On the first day, after all the participants had taken their seats, one of Erhard's staff would begin by reading out a long list of rules. The participants were not allowed to leave their seats, not even to go to the bathroom (other than during short breaks). Drinking and eating weren't allowed. They started at 9 a.m. and continued at least until midnight, sometimes as long as 4 a.m. They had only one break for meals.

And so, after the assistant had read out the rules, Erhard stormed into the room, grabbed a microphone and began with the following evocative words:

IN THIS TRAINING, YOU'RE GOING TO FIND OUT YOU'VE BEEN ACTING LIKE ASSHOLES. ALL YOUR FUCKING CLEVERNESS AND SELF-DECEPTION HAVE GOTTEN YOU NOWHERE.[12]

The start was intense. It consisted of hour-long sessions of verbal insults. The participants were told that they were 'all worthless human beings who clung to beliefs about themselves and their own lives that were rooted in ridiculous notions about reason, logic, and understanding'.[13]

It was a long day indeed, and by the end of the fifteen-hour training, all participants were lying down on the floor, eyes closed, immersed in meditation tasks, referred to as 'processes'. Ostensibly, it enabled the participants to 'create their own experience'.[14]

Day two was dedicated to truth. Here, Erhard employed the methods he had picked up from his previous engagements with Scientology and Mind Dynamics. It could be described as a mass psychotherapy session, where all of the participants would lie down on the floor, eyes closed, and concentrate on a particular item that they wanted to free themselves from. In a process inspired by the techniques of Fritz Perls, the participants were asked to travel back in time and search through the dark corners of their memory, thereby tracking down and identifying those irritating items that they most wanted to get rid of. In his essay on narcissism, Wolfe went to est. He described how people cried and screamed as they confronted their demons. Others threw up. Vomit bags weree available. A woman started moaning: 'Ooooooooooooooohhhhhhhhhhhh!' 'And when she starts moaning,' Wolfe continued, 'the most incredible and exhilarating thing begins to happen. A wave of moans spreads through the people lying around her, as if her energy were radiating out like a radar pulse.' She then let her 'keening sound' turn into a real scream, like she had never screamed before, and then her full scream spread 'from soul to soul, over top of the keens and fading moans'.[15]

The second day ended with a series of exercises called 'bullbaiting', 'confronting', and 'danger process', where trainees first had to climb the stage and, face-to-face with one of Erhard's staff, receive a barrage of insults. They then had to lie down on the carpet, imagining they were morbidly afraid of all other people. And at this point, as they had been pushed to the point of a nervous breakdown, came the long-awaited turn of events. They had to imagine that everyone else was afraid of *them*. At this point, a sense of relief supposedly emerged, with the realization that fear was purely imaginary, a construction inside their heads, which they could rid themselves of.

One week later, the same crowd gathered for the third day of training, consisting of a series of long lectures delivered by Erhard. Drawing on a dizzy array of sources, he delivered his idiosyncratic philosophy, meant to provoke the audience to dramatically rethinking what they had previously thought to be real and unreal. The fourth and final day continued with a long lecture that could go on for up to ten hours, culminating in the wisdom that: 'You are what you are, and you are responsible for everything you do.'[16]

est became an immensely popular training programme, but not all of the participants were satisfied. When one person was asked if he had learnt anything in the training, he said yes, 'I learned to stand in front of 250 people and say you're nothing but a bunch of fucking assholes.'[17] But the training was cleverly designed to make the participants feel included. Everyone passed the test and would eventually 'get it', especially those who were struggling to understand the point at the outset. 'Did you get it?' they were asked by the end of the four-day training. Many would approvingly raise their arms, saying that they'd comprehended the message. But usually there were more people in the audience who would say that they had not 'gotten it'. 'Good,' was the reply they received in a pseudo-Wittgensteinian turn. 'There's nothing to get so you got it.'[18]

In 1975, the journalist Peter Marin published an article in *Harper's* magazine called 'The New Narcissism' in which he warned against the emergence of a new type of solipsistic culture 'centred solely on the self and with individual survival as its sole good'. Marin recounts a dinner conversation with a woman who had recently come back from a weekend training at est. She said 'her life had radically changed, that she felt different about herself, that she was happier and more efficient, and that she kept her house much cleaner than before'. At the seminar, she had learnt:

'(1) that the individual will is all-powerful and totally determines one's fate; (2) that she felt neither guilt nor shame about anyone's fate and that those who were poor and hungry must have wished it on themselves'.[19] Marin lists seven more insights that the woman had gained during her stay at est. Among these, she had learnt that the North Vietnamese had wanted to be bombed; that a friend of hers who had been raped and murdered also had wished it upon herself; that she had now become fully enlightened, a sort of god; and that whatever you *think* is true *is* true, because reason is irrational. Finally, she told Marin that he, too, had to go to est.

The purpose of est was to help people become free from the emotional constraints they imposed on themselves. They learnt how to stop being slaves under external circumstances. To use the terminology of Wilhelm Reich, they were instructed to kill the 'little man' inside and grow up to take ownership over their own lives. 'I'm afraid of you, little man, very much afraid,' Reich wrote. 'You're sick, little man, very sick. It's not your fault; but it's your responsibility to get well.'[20] Reich claimed that the little man fails to take responsibility for his own actions. He is sexually frustrated and lacks the courage to live an authentic life. The little man is constantly afraid, both of himself and of others. In Erhard's training, the participants were, as he put it, untrained to be afraid. They had to unlearn how to be a little man. By the end of the training, their experience of living should have transformed, so that 'the situations you have been trying to change or have been putting up with clear up just in the process of life itself'.[21]

But this insistence on individual responsibility reached grotesque depths. Pressman describes how, in one est session:

> Erhard set about convincing a Holocaust survivor and est participant that she – along with family members who had perished in a Nazi death camp – was 'responsible' for her own predicament. Neither the Nazis nor Hitler, Erhard said later, created the woman's 'experience' of the concentration camp. They were only an illusion. The reality, said Erhard, was that she had created her Holocaust experience.[22]

When asked by one of the participants what the woman could have done to avoid her fate, Erhard answered, somewhat puzzlingly, 'How could the light be off when it's turned on? The question is completely stupid.'[23]

During the 1970s, as people flocked to training pro-grammes such as est, the happiness fantasy took on a new meaning. Reich's insistence on authentic selfhood and sexual liberation, which had been picked up in the Sixties as a radical idea in the struggle against state oppression, had now been repackaged as a route to personal liberation and financial success. The purpose was to liberate the individual from all their mental constructions. All individuals were free to be who they wanted to be. They could always do what Erhard had done, and change names and jump on a plane. He was the living proof that it was possible to change one's life. Since there were no constraints apart from their mental constructions, the participants had no legitimate reasons to feel sorry for anyone, especially not themselves.

More than a route towards personal liberation, the notion of a world without victims is central to the neoliberal fantasy, according to which all people have the same opportunities to become happy and successful regardless of their circumstances. It is a notion that is just as popular with right-wing politicians such as Donald Trump as it is with self-help gurus such as Oprah Winfrey.

## The Cruelty of Inspirational Messages

In the summer of 2015, while walking past a McDonald's restaurant in the Philippines, a medical student, Joyce Torrefranca, spotted a young boy sitting outside doing his homework at an improvised table. It was late in the evening, but the boy could read and write using the lights coming from the nearby restaurant. Moved by the scene, Torrefranca took a photograph and posted it on Facebook. 'For me as a student,' she wrote, 'it just hit me a lot, like, big time.'

This was the perfect image of the happiness fantasy. Daniel Cabrera was a nine-year-old boy without a home. After his house burnt down, he had lived in a food stall with his mother and two brothers. His father was dead. Reports also said that he owned only one pencil. He used to have two, but the second pencil was stolen from him.

Torrefranca wasn't the only one inspired by this story. As it went viral, people came forward to help the boy in whatever way they could. He received books, pencils, and crayons. Someone gave him a battery-powered lamp so he would no longer have to do his homework in the car park. A fundraising page was set up to help cover the costs of his schooling.

But, for some, the story also carried an important moral message: that to succeed in life, will-power and determination are absolutely key. It was the same kind of message that was promoted by Werner Erhard at est. There are no victims in the world. Our lives are never predetermined. No matter how bad the circumstances, it is our responsibility to create our own lives.

One English tabloid newspaper thought that the picture could be used for educational purposes. It encouraged parents to show the picture of the hardworking boy to their children next time they moaned or complained. In a similar vein, someone turned the picture into an inspirational online postcard with the motivational caption: 'If it is important to you, you will find a way. If not, you'll find an excuse.'

In this context, when paired with inspirational messages, the picture attains a new meaning, as a reminder that there are no excuses for failure or poverty. Even if you are poor and live in a makeshift home, you have the choice to work yourself out of that predicament. All you need is determination, will-power, and the right, can-do attitude.

The message that Erhard spread to 700,000 people during the 1970s and 1980s was that we are responsible for everything that happens to us, including such circumstances as having our homes burnt down or being destined to live in a makeshift house on the street. 'From illness and disease to auto accidents and street muggings,' Pressman writes about Erhard and the message he conveyed through est, 'they alone caused all the incidents and episodes in their lives to occur.' There was 'no room for victims or excuses. Only when his customers accepted that, only when they realized that all people "create their own reality", were they in a position to resolve problems plaguing their lives.'[24]

Erhard's ideas are influential to this day. While est formally closed down in 1985, it continued under the name Forum, and still operates today, under the brand Landmark Worldwide. This training programme has been popular with celebrities such as Steven Spielberg, Barbra Streisand, Cher, and Elizabeth Taylor. It has also been popular with today's self-help queen, Oprah Winfrey, who promotes a message that is remarkably similar to that of Erhard.

In *The New Prophets of Capital*, Nicole Aschoff describes how Oprah, in 1994, declared that she wanted to add a more positive feel to her popular television show. Instead of only focusing on what was wrong in people's lives, she wanted to present constructive strategies to help people rise as human beings. 'It's time to move on from "We are dysfunctional" to "What are we going to do about it?"'

In an attempt at making her show more positive, Oprah turned to the spiritual self-help guru Marianne Williamson for inspiration. When she appeared on the show to explain her message, Williamson used the example of a depressed mother who lived on welfare. She was suffering from an inability to 'let go of her "victim mentality"' and lacked the courage to embrace the notion that 'I have within me the power to break through these constrictions.' In another episode, a young single mother appeared to explain that she had now, after watching a previous *Oprah* show, understood that being fired was not a problem. It was something for which she should be grateful. On hearing this, Oprah remarked: 'Any time you get fired, you should say thank you.'[25]

Like Erhard, Oprah promotes a classic self-help message, which can be traced at least as far back as to the work of Napoleon Hill. 'There are millions of people,' Hill wrote in *Think and Grow Rich*, published in 1936, 'who believe themselves "doomed" to poverty and failure, because of some strange force over which they believe they have no control. They are the creators of their own "misfortunes", because of this negative belief.'[26]

When Oprah brings this message into her show, she does it in a deliberately feminine and compassionate manner. Being laid off is not a problem; it is an opportunity to grow as a human being. Losing one's job could be the necessary push to discover and tap one's inner potentials. As Aschoff suggests, Oprah is one of the new prophets of capital precisely because she connects an individualistic self-help ethos with the logic of capital, in which the individual, as an obedient neoliberal agent, takes an active role in her own exploitation, meanwhile pretending as though these activities are perfectly attuned with her inner desire – as an expression of her own quest for authenticity.

But there is an interesting paradox at play here: while asked to turn the gaze inwards and discover one's inner resources, the neoliberal agent is also asked to look outwards for places to sell and promote their resources. Living in the age of capital, we have infinite possibilities hidden inside us insofar as there are infinite possibilities of making them valuable by turning them into commodities. And being fired may help you come to that realization. As Philip Mirowski wryly remarks in his book *Never Let a Serious Crisis Go to Waste:* 'Unemployment is an unbidden golden opportunity to start anew with an entirely different life! Don't let the moochers and complainers drag you down! Become your own boss, after you embrace the power of positive thinking ... Didn't you always want to start your own business, after working a quarter-century for corporations?'[27] Behind our mental constraints, there are endless possibilities. But to find them we need to stop seeing ourselves as victims. In the October 2013 issue of Oprah's magazine, unemployed people were instructed to look for their hidden talents and harness their 'onlyness' and nurture their 'kick-ass individuality'.

We can see here how the happiness fantasy has been transmuted into a version of the neoliberal fantasy. Huxley's dream of human potentiality, as he expressed it at the beginning of the 1960s, was a dream in which people, irrespective of their constitution, could develop their inner potentials and blossom as human beings. Today, the only differences that are tolerated are those that can be commodified and rendered valuable.

## We Are All Narcissists Now

On the cover of *Time* magazine from 20 May 2013, we see a young woman lying on her stomach taking a selfie. The caption reads 'The Me Me Me Generation'.

A covert wink to Tom Wolfe's 1976 article, this cover piece portrayed millennials as lazy and entitled narcissists. It implied that the Me Decade of the 1970s had returned, three decades later, in the form of the internet-based Me Generation. But was it fair to equate these two types of narcissists?

Not according to the Facebook activists who responded with an array of creative memes in which the original text was altered to better fit with the reality of millennials. One version replaced 'The Me Me Me Generation' with 'The Unemployed Generation'. Another one read 'The Doomed Generation'. The new captions claimed that millennials now found themselves in hopeless situations, with large amounts of student debts, inflated housing rents, and bleak prospects of finding decent work. 'Millennials are narcissists because we fucked their entire generation over and they don't have anything better to do than jerk off and look at Tumblr,' one meme read. Another one: 'We pissed their future away on endless wars, golden parachutes for bankers, and hand jobs for stockbrokers.'

I found the original cover distasteful and the responding memes fairly amusing, but I never really thought about it seriously until years later, when I was going to teach a course on a related topic, and thought it a good idea to show the cover to my students.

I handed out photocopies of the cover and asked if they thought it to be an accurate description of their situation. Instead of the outburst I had expected, my students responded with a collective shrug of the shoulders.

'It's sort of accurate, I guess,' one student said.

'Look, we *are* narcissists,' another one added.

'You know,' a third student began, 'as we grew up, we were all told how wonderfully special we were.' Many of the other students in the room nodded. They had all been told the same things. And they all knew it was a lie. As the student went on to explain, even though the injunction today is to become a celebrity, as Sheila Heti writes in the epigraph to this chapter, they weren't so stupid as to seriously believe they would all grow up to become celebrities like the Kardashians, Justin Bieber, or Paris Hilton.

Then one student protested. She explained that she, too, had been told that she was special. But she had also been told that, unless she worked really hard in school and achieved great results, she would stand no chance in competing with the Chinese. The remark had an unpleasant ring. There were some Chinese students in the room. I looked their way. They smiled back, stoically.

In *The Culture of Narcissism*, from 1979, Christopher Lasch writes that the 'narcissist admires and identifies himself with "winners"'.[28]

But my students didn't seem to be talking about self-love or auto-eroticism. They didn't see themselves as the winners. When they called themselves narcissistic, they meant it in a fatalistic manner. They seemed to think of narcissism not as a personality trait, but as a set of culturally contingent characteristics that they were required to display. Their narcissism was not by choice, but by necessity. Since then, I've been thinking about them as a generation of compulsory narcissists. On the one hand, they are expected to present themselves in a favourable light. They have to demonstrate to the outer world that they are ambitious and special, reaching for the stars, as though they are some kind of celebrity. On the other hand, they are constantly reminded that the reality they are about to encounter is harsh and that they are required to develop an elaborately competitive mind-set.

Which is why it is unfair, and simply wrong-headed, to call them narcissists. One is not suffering from a disorder on the basis of embracing the cultural values that are esteemed by society. We all know that the first question a millennial receives today when applying for a job is what makes them stand out from the crowd. In an age of Oprah, millennials are expected to style themselves as kick-ass individuals – young entrepreneurial souls with a longing for branding who are trained in the art of displaying their 'onlyness'. Meanwhile, they are well aware that they aren't unique. They simply have to play along. How else could they stand out from the crowd?

To appreciate the difference between the compulsory narcissists in my class and the voluntary narcissists described by Wolfe, we need to acknowledge that young people today face a harsher reality than they did in the 1970s with regard to finding stable employment and affordable housing. The compulsory narcissists came of age in the midst of the financial crisis. Their lives have been defined not by affluence and abundance, as was the case with the narcissists described by Wolfe, but by precarity, austerity, and student debts. They cannot afford to turn their backs on the world, because the world will turn its back on them first.

Meanwhile, many young people are expected not just to follow their dreams, but to create and endorse their own trademark while doing so. Compulsory narcissists are required to believe in the myth of meritocracy and think of themselves as winners.

To this end, they have to manipulate what they know about politics and economics. They have to cease thinking of unemployment as a political affair, and regard it as an individual defect. We find an uncanny example of this in Ivor Southwood's auto-ethnographic account of UK jobcentres, *Non-Stop Inertia*, where jobseekers are told to do 'three positive things per week' or else they will get disciplined.[29] As argued in a recently published article in the journal *Critical Medical Humanities*,[30] these types of exercises, intended to modify attitudes, beliefs, and personality, have become a political strategy aimed to eradicate the experience of social and economic inequality.

This was the desired outcome of seminar trainings such as those provided by est. By the end of the training, the participants were supposed to believe that circumstances were mere illusions. People's lives were not shaped by their social background or their economic resources but purely by their own minds.

## The Modern Confession

'We are all narcissists now,' one of my students continued. They had started to talk about their social media habits. 'I mean, just look at the pictures we post on Facebook and

Instagram,' they went on, telling me more than I wanted to know about their experiences of sharing.

'Sharing' was a central activity at both Esalen and est, but the moral obligation to reveal intimate details about oneself goes back much further than that. In *The History of Sexuality*, from 1976, the philosopher Michel Foucault points out that the confession is the ritual on which religious and civil society has relied since the Middle Ages. Its function, according to Foucault, is to produce truth, and to directly implicate the subject into that process. He writes that the 'obligation to confess' is now 'so deeply ingrained in us, that we no longer perceive it as the effect of a power that constrains us'. We seem to think that the truths that are hidden inside us need to come out. If we fail to let these truths surface, we have revealed our inability to be free.[31]

In the 1970s, as hundreds of thousands of Americans attended training programmes to discover themselves, the confession came to play a central role in their pursuit to gain autonomy and freedom. Participants were asked to confront their inner demons, fight against internalized authority figures, and liberate themselves from externally imposed constraints. They were asked to reconnect with their inner self and hand themselves over to enjoyment, and, to this end, the confession played a central role.

Recall the hotel ballroom that Tom Wolfe described in his essay about narcissism. The scene is from the third day of the est training, when all of the participants were asked to announce one item that they wanted to eliminate from their lives. People entered the scene to announce what they wanted to free themselves of. One woman climbed the stage and grabbed the microphone to *share* her secret. She didn't want to eliminate her self-destructiveness or laziness, as other people wished. No, she wanted to eliminate her haemorrhoids.

The participants had now identified the items they wanted to get rid of. The trainer asked them to 'lie down on the floor and close their eyes and get deep into their own spaces and concentrate on that one item they wanted to get rid of the most – and really feel it and let the feeling gush out'. So there she was, on the floor, properly *feeling* her haemorrhoids – 'the sensation', as Wolfe put it, 'that a peanut was caught in her anal sphincter'.

The purpose of these workshops was to become liberated from the 'excess baggage of society' and 'find the Real Me'. But in order for that to happen, the individual had to let go and 'take the finger off the repress-button' and reveal their innermost secrets. They were encouraged to talk about themselves at great length and with no shame. They were instructed to speak out in front of the other participants, even if they were in the hundreds.

Today, as the hotel ballroom has been replaced by the internet, we are able to share our secrets with more than just a few hundreds.

In 2006, at the age of twenty-four, the blogger Emily Gould was offered a job at Gawker, a gossip blog aimed at revealing the assumed double life of celebrities and to expose their secrets – whether or not they had any. In the world according to Gawker, Gould explained in an article for the *New York Times*: 'Everyone was fatter or older or worse-skinned than he or she pretended to be. Every man was cheating on his partner; all women were slutty. Writers were plagiarists or talentless hacks or shameless beneficiaries of nepotism. Everyone was a hypocrite.'[32]

Gawker was a pioneering actor in what the philosopher Byung-Chul Han has called a society of transparency,[33] a society in which all private secrets are made public. While the readers of Gawker were protected behind their screens, the writers, like Gould, were not. They, too, became subjected to the scrutinizing eyes of the readers. When Gould first started, her editor had advised her not to read the comments. But she couldn't resist the temptation. The commenters weren't friends, Gould explains. 'It was almost something deeper':

> They were co-workers, sort of, giving me ideas for posts, rewriting my punch lines. They were creeps hitting on me at a bar. They were fans, sycophantically praising even my lamer efforts. They were enemies, articulating my worst fears about my limitations. They were the voices in my head. They could be ignored sometimes. Or, if I let them, they could become my whole world.[34]

The voice of the readers, being so close that they sometimes wormed themselves into her head, played a central part in what and how she wrote. The readers always asked her to write more about herself, revealing as many intimate details as possible. They wanted her to confess the naked truth about herself. The more personal and emotional she was, the more views and likes she received. She wrote about sex, her desire to kill her mother (whom she also loved more than anyone else), and her urinary tract infection.

While the participants at est had to stand up and *share* their secrets with 250 other people in a room, all of whom were engaged in the same training, bloggers such as Gould spoke in front of an anonymous mass of hundreds of thousands (sometimes millions), all of whom were safely hidden behind screens.

If she didn't know who these people were, then for whom did she confess? Was it merely for her own sake? Foucault reminds us that the confession is a ritual that 'unfolds within a power relationship' and that there is always some kind of 'authority who requires the confession'.[35]

Power and authority are rarely mentioned when talking about 'sharing'. Consider the workshops at Esalen in which individuals were instructed to confront their own fears and limitations. Perls didn't see himself as an authority figure and he didn't see his workshops as producing and exercising power. Instead he saw them as processes by which individuals were liberated from power relations and constraints.

But this is a very naïve notion of power. Since its emergence in the work of Reich, the happiness fantasy has been based on the optimistic belief that personal freedom and authentic selfhood are gained through the renunciation of authority figures. This is a naïve notion because power emerges not only in visible authority figures or in the form of prohibition. When Reich asked his patients to become liberated, he implicated the patients in a different form of power relation, which could be just as imposing as traditional forms of exercising power. Getting on Perls's hot seat and revealing one's inner fears was also producing a form of power relation in which the individual was made extremely vulnerable. As Gould continued to expose secrets on her blog, she was both lauded and punished by the readers. Like the person on Perls's hot seat, she was encouraged to expose her inner life to an audience. But rather than making her free and liberated, this form of public confession only made her more defenceless and vulnerable.

Gould participated in a culture of narcissism that she knew was harmful, and I would argue that this is a fate she shares with all compulsory narcissists, who are engaged in forms of self-promotion not because they necessarily want to, but because they have to. They are trained to turn their idiosyncrasies into competitive advantages and to share their personal experiences and demonstrate their ability to work hard and market themselves. The world they have inhabited is defined by notions of relentless competition and individualism. If they fail to make it on the job market, it is their responsibility to figure out why. Could they have done more to promote themselves, or worked harder to display their unique selling points, or spent more time and effort on cultivating their innate talents?

Such is the cruel fate of the compulsory narcissists. They are doomed to examine themselves, not according to philosophical principles in a spirit of wonder, but according to financial principles in a spirit of self-critique.

It is no small irony to note that Reich's fantasy of happiness no longer stands in opposition to power and domination, but is used as a way of exercising power and domination. As I will argue in the next chapter, this irony is nowhere more evident than in the contemporary workplace, where the fantasy of happiness is continuously and ingeniously employed to exploit workers.

# 3

# Happiness Inc.

That's when I first learned that it wasn't enough to just do your
job, you had to have an interest in it, even a passion for it.

Charles Bukowski, *Factotum*[1]

## Be Yourself and Have Fun

For Tony Hsieh, the CEO of Zappos, a bet is a bet. When
graduating from Harvard, he made the following wager
with his friends: if he became a millionaire within the next
ten years, he would invite all of them on a cruise. In 1999,
after selling his first company to Microsoft, he had indeed
become a millionaire, and so invited his friends on a three-
day cruise to the Bahamas. 'In the eyes of all my friends on
the cruise,' Hsieh boasts in his self-indulgent success story
*Delivering Happiness*, 'I was everything that they thought
defined success and happiness.' But as he was standing
there, in the night club on the cruise with a drink in his

hand, a nagging voice in the back of his head asked, 'What is success? What is happiness? What am I working towards?'[2]

Shortly after his return, Hsieh made a list of the happiest periods in his life, and realized that none of them involved money. What made him happy was building stuff, being creative, spending time with friends, and eating the food he liked (baked potato and pickles, we learn). 'I thought about how easily we are all brainwashed by our society and culture to stop thinking and just assume by default that more money equals more success and more happiness, when ultimately happiness is really just about enjoying life.'

This was on the eve of the new millennium, and he realized that there would never be another 1999. He decided it was time to be 'true to myself'. He resigned from his uninspiring and dull office work at Microsoft. 'I didn't know exactly what I was going to do, but I knew what I wasn't going to do. I wasn't going to sit around letting my life and the world pass me by.'

He moved into a loft with some friends, converted one of the bedrooms to an office, set up an investment fund, and then chanced upon the idea of selling shoes over the internet. It was a huge industry and catalogue sales made up 2 billion. And so, Zappos was born.

After a few testing years, Zappos had become a profitable company, and now had to construct a more solid identity. Influenced by the business guru Jim Collins and his book Good to Great, Hsieh believed that to become truly great it first had to discover its real identity. What made Zappos different from other companies, he realized after discussing the issue with his colleagues, was its genuine and innovative way with customers. Zappos, of course, would have the world's leading customer service. Its vision: 'delivering happiness to customers, employees, and vendors'.

Determined to become the best customer service in the world, it moved from San Francisco to Las Vegas, a relocation that didn't seem wise financially, but made perfect sense culturally. Las Vegas, Hsieh believed, was a place where his employees would be happy. And the group of people who went there together would no doubt become tight, because they knew no other people in Las Vegas. Hsieh realized that to pull this off, Zappos needed a strong culture. From now on, culture was the number one priority.

Zappos has since become an iconic company, known especially for its spectacular culture, which people from the outside are invited to witness as part of their official tour. Visitors are allowed to enter the premises and observe the culture first hand, to *experience* the company's energetic atmosphere.

In the 1980s and 1990s, American corporations began to consider the notion of culture more seriously. Management gurus had listened carefully to the complaints from managers. They didn't know what to do with their moaning employees. They seemed disgruntled and unmotivated. The business gurus explained that people needed to feel passionate about what they do. They needed a sense of belonging and a strong identity. And most importantly, the employees needed to feel that work was not just something they did, but something through which they could actualize their true inner selves.

The human potential movement, with seminar programmes such as est, had spread rapidly during the 1970s,
and it was to these movements that some of the more pro-
gressive business leaders now directed their attention. This
may seem an ironic turn of events. When the fantasy of
happiness emerged in the Sixties countercultures, it did
so in opposition to corporations and social institutions.
But then, in the 1970s, as this fantasy became sold to large
parts of the rapidly growing middle classes, it no longer
had a distinct political orientation. And then, in the 1980s,
corporations slowly began to take note, exploring more
unconventional ideas, including those of the New Age. As
the *Wall Street Journal* reported in 1987: 'Dozens of major
US companies – including Ford Motor Co, Proctor &
Gamble Co, TRW Inc., Polaroid Corp., and Pacific Telesis
Group Inc. – are spending millions of dollars on so-called
New Age workshops.'[3]

And so, in the early 1990s, Michael Murphy, the
co-founder of Esalen, began an initiative aimed at attract-
ing more businesses to its premises in Big Sur. As a first
step, he turned one of its buildings into a corporate retreat,
where trainees were offered courses in personal growth,
stress reduction, and creativity enhancement. Trainees
who came there were not just trained to take ownership
over their own life. They also had to take '"ownership" over
the company's result'.[4]

As companies started to engage more promiscuously
with New Age movements, adopting and subsequently
co-opting the vocabulary of human transformation and
individual freedom, they became more appealing to bands

of freethinking individuals who had previously shunned corporate powers like the plague. 'In the Sixties these people would have slit their wrists before walking into any institution of corporate America,' the business books editor at Doubleday, Harriet Rubin, explained in an interview from 1990. 'Now corporations are seen as a sort of living laboratory for their ideas.'[5]

In the same article, published in *Fortune*, Frank Rose described the emergence of a new age of business, where business leaders had replaced their obsession with numbers with a more open-minded vision about human potential. Rose describes how Levi Strauss & Co, among other corporations, had tuned itself into this new frequency. Chairman Robert Haas had just announced his vision of the corporation as a kind of global enterprise consisting of creative people who 'are able to tap their fullest potential'. Meanwhile, managers should no longer act as paternal authority figures. Instead, he explained, they should act as 'coaches, facilitators, and role models'.[6] As a fashion company, Levi Strauss had to be receptive to new trends. Or better still, it had to attract the creative types who were setting the new trends. Levi Strauss was not alone in subjecting itself to these forms of extreme makeovers. Microsoft adopted an almost identical mantra, stating as its vision: 'To enable people and business throughout the world to realize their full potential.'[7]

Unsurprisingly Werner Erhard, as the leader of the human transformation movement, had won lucrative personnel-training contracts from such major corporations as

TRW Automotive and Ford.[8] In 1984, to adapt himself to the new climate, he changed the name of his training from est to Forum, which gave it a more professional feel and made it more business-minded.

Erhard continued to run Forum until 1991, when, amidst allegations of sexual molestation and tax fraud (of which he was later found innocent), he sold his 'technologies' on to his closest colleagues, one of whom was his brother, Harry Rosenberg. They altered the name to Landmark Forum and continued Erhard's ongoing ambition to make the training more suitable to those aspiring towards a successful career. As the historian Suzanne Snider writes:

> Since est evolved into the Forum, so has the audience for such 'technologies' evolved – from New Age hippies to CEOs to CEO-hippy hybrids – a transformation that provides a lesson not only about corporate identity re-branding and our culture's shifting standards of legitimacy; it also suggests what we dream about thirty years later, when we dream about our own potential.[9]

Landmark Forum is still in operation today, and by accessing its website, we can read about its training programmes, which are aimed at bringing about 'positive, permanent shifts in the quality of your life', which will make the trainee 'experience a new and unique kind of freedom, effectiveness, and power – the freedom to be at ease in any circumstance, a new effectiveness in areas that really matter to you, and the power to make what you're committed to into a reality'.[10]

The training is still popular with corporations. One of the most vocal supporters of Landmark is the yoga apparel company lululemon, which, like est, should be written in lower-case. In an article published in the *Evening Standard*, a community manager at lululemon described the company as more than just a place where you go to buy 'hotty hot shorts'.[11] 'We have a very strong culture and are a value-based company. Our mission is to elevate the world from mediocrity to greatness.' Sales assistants are called 'educators' and customers 'guests'. All employees are asked to publicly announce their ten-year goals, and after one year at the company they are invited to undergo the three-day Landmark training, free of charge.

In the 1980s, business gurus began promoting a new type of managerial strategy. Developing strong corporate cultures, managers could motivate their employees in more effective and profound ways. If employees could be persuaded that they weren't simply working for the money, but for something larger than themselves, they could be brought into the corporation in a more emotionally and socially encompassing manner, as members of a family. The aspiration was to replace compliance with commitment, motivating the employees to invest their time and energy into developing the company. They would not merely come into the office and comply to the rules, as working robots. They would come there with their thoughts, beliefs, experiences, feelings, and creative powers – all of which were now considered vital resources in enriching the value of the organization.

The ingenious part of this strategy was that, by making employees feel more integrated into the culture, they no longer had to be controlled or motivated in punitive or technocratic terms. Targeting the emotional aspect of the employees made it possible to control them in what appeared to be a more benign manner. This form of control, which the organization scholar Gideon Kunda has called normative, is based 'on an experiential transaction, one in which symbolic rewards are exchanged for a moral orientation to the organization'.[12] Employees are addressed not just as employees, but as their own individual *selves*.

'I've never dealt with a company that is so positive,' a yoga studio owner told the *Evening Standard* when asked about lululemon. 'The word "meeting" is banned, you say "connect" instead, and the main aim of each connect is to "surprise and delight".'

In his book *Authenticity and the Cultural Politics of Work*, management professor Peter Fleming describes an Australian call centre, called Sunray, in which employees were urged to exhibit their true selves, warts and all. Employees could bring personal items to work. There were no dress codes. Parties were arranged and sexual relationships between colleagues were permitted. When one woman was left by her boyfriend, she was asked to turn up to work and share her experiences and emotions. As Fleming remarks, the injunction at this workplace was not to be someone else, but an injunction to 'just be yourself'.[13]

In a *New York Times* profile of Zappos, we find a similar description: 'The youthful work force is heavily tattooed; the dress code is aggressively casual. Desks are cluttered with giant stuffed animals, and sound-emitting sculptures designed by the Blue Man Group line the walls.'[14] When Tony Hsieh decided to make culture his number one priority, he did not want to impose his own ideas. Instead he asked all of the staff to write down what Zappos was for *them*. The result was the Zappos Culture book, which lists the employees' various *experiences*, and summarizes the ten core values of the company, one of which is to 'create fun and a little weirdness'. Ask yourself, Hsieh writes, 'what can we do to be a little weird and differentiate ourselves from everyone else?'[15]

When visitors come to Zappos's offices for one of the 'culture tours', they are able to experience this weirdness themselves. 'Every tour is different,' Hsieh explains in *Delivering Happiness.* 'You might find a popcorn machine or a coffee machine dressed up as a robot in our lobby.' You might find 'a makeshift bowling alley built by our software developers, employees dressed up as pirates, employees karaokeing, a nap room a petting zoo, or a hot dog social'. He continues: 'Or you might happen to show up during our annual "Bald & Blue" day, where employees volunteer to get their heads shaved by other employees.' The quirkiness and craziness are, of course, part of a more encompassing ideology of work. On their website, Zappos explains:

> We encourage you to be yourself and have fun. We don't promote work/life balance in the traditional sense, rather we believe in 'work/life integration'. We like having a good time at work, not just outside of it. There's no need to hide your random quirks or awkward dance moves from us. In a way, you might be taking a 'break from life' by working here!

The anti-authoritarian ideals, as they were first organized collectively as a response against corporate America, have now become fully integrated into corporate cultures such as Zappos, lululemon, and Sunray. When Reich developed his notion of happiness based on the moral values of authenticity and sexuality, he could never have dreamed of finding these values in the context of the workplace.

How did we come to this point? Why are so many organizations now engaged in promoting a message of personal freedom and happiness? To understand this cultural shift, we need to go back in time and consider the critique that was levelled in the 1950s and 1960s against wage labour and work organizations. Back then, there was nothing cool or liberating about going to work in the morning and returning home in the evening. For the Beat generation of the 1950s, wage labour was a mind-numbing evil that killed authenticity and creativity. And for the students who took to the streets in the late 1960s, work was a prison that one had to escape from.

## The Beat Corporation

Charles Bukowski was many things – a poet, a novelist, a pickle factory worker, a postman, a drunk – but he surely wasn't a poster boy for glowing happiness. Bukowski's retreating eyes and scarred face, with deep lines slanting from his nostrils, were no doubt a product of the long nights spent drinking in rundown bars. But that was not the only thing that wore him down. There was something else to blame too, and that was work – hard menial labour.

In 1969, at the age of forty-nine, Bukowski was finally able to escape the prison of wage labor. In a letter to his publisher John Martin, who, by offering a monthly salary of $100, had made this exit possible, Bukowski described what a terrible blow work had dealt him.

'The color leaves the eye. The voice becomes ugly. And the body. The hair. The fingernails. The shoes.'

Why, asked Bukowski, would anyone agree to such humiliation? 'As a young man', he wrote in the same letter, 'I could not believe that people could give their lives over to those conditions. As an old man, I still can't believe it. What do they do it for? Sex? TV? An automobile on monthly payments? Or children? Children who are just going to do the same things that they did?'[16]

Bukowski was not alone in feeling this way. At first, when big corporations like the Ford Motor Company had ushered in a whole new structure of life, with a sharp divide between work and leisure, it looked like a humane breakthrough. The forty-hour workweek, institutionalized in 1938 as part of the Fair Labor Standard Act, was a definite step up from the harsh conditions of industrialism where work seemed to go on, non-stop, from dawn to dusk.

But the mood had changed quickly, and by the time of the 1950s and 1960s, as bohemians settled in California, and Beats and hippies came to the cultural fore, 9-to-5 drudgery had become a symbol of the inauthentic life, a constant and pointless shuttling between the office and the television set. It seems somewhat ironic: the critique that was levelled by countercultural groups in the 1950s and 1960s has now resulted in the image of Zappos and 'work–life integration'. Roughly sixty years down the line, we have achieved a new type of precarious 24/7 work culture. Whatever the Beats and the hippies dreamt of, it was not this.

In the mid-1950s, while living in San Francisco, the poet Allen Ginsberg had found a job in market research. Even though this was exactly the kind of job he had been looking for, he feared that it would enslave him. Asked by his therapist what he most wanted to do, Ginsberg replied, 'I really would like to stop working forever – never work again, never do anything like the kind of work I'm doing now – and do nothing but write poetry and have leisure to spend the day outdoors and go to museums and see friends.'[17]

For Ginsberg's close friend William S. Burroughs, who, apart from styling himself as an outlaw, also received an allowance from his parents, wage labour was never really a serious option. When asked by the *Paris Review* in its Fall 1965 issue why he started taking drugs, Burroughs wryly replied, 'Well, I was just bored. I didn't seem to have much interest in becoming a successful advertising executive or whatever.'

It was also at around this time, in the mid-1960s, that Wilhelm Reich became posthumously famous. He was widely embraced as a countercultural icon, and one of his many enthusiasts was Burroughs, who had acquired numerous orgone accumulators. In a letter to Kerouac from 1949, explaining his successful experiments with the orgone box, Burroughs wrote: 'The man is not crazy, he's a fucking genius.'[18]

Reich's distinctly anti-authoritarian message of sexual emancipation and social change struck a chord in the last years of the 1960s, as student revolts were spreading across the world. His critique of authority, paternalism, and the structure of the family had gone mainstream. The utopian visions expressed by the Beats were heard from shouting crowds. And on the streets of Paris, protesters were writing anti-work slogans, 'commute, work, commute, sleep…', 'You will all end up dying from comfort', and 'Never work'. In *The Revolution of Everyday Life*, the situationist Raoul Vaneigem, a central figure of the 1968 uprising, launched an attack against the conformist life, divided between work and leisure, two activities which he likened to 'the twin blades of castrating shears'.[19] After the revolution, he fancied, strikers would demand ten-hour weeks, stop picketing, and start making love in factories and offices.

But this, of course, is not how things turned out. It is true that self-styled gurus such as Tim Ferriss like to talk about four-hour workweeks, and other entrepreneurial delusions, but that kind of diagnosis is hard to take seriously at a time when the average full-time American is working more than forty hours a week. How could we explain this development? In the years following the 1968 uprisings, people continued to express their discontent with work. Mass strikes in France and elsewhere forced employers to respond to the critique. Their initial strategy was to negotiate better salaries and improve job security with unions, but that method proved futile.

In the second half of the 1970s, some employers changed tactics. If all these people cared about was freedom, autonomy, and authenticity, then why not give it to them? Or, rather, why not proclaim that you were giving it to them?

This became the start of what the French theorists Luc Boltanski and Ève Chiapello call a new spirit of capitalism.[20] Words such as solidarity, equality, and security were considered out of date. The state became an object of suspicion. And bureaucratic institutions and Fordist work structures became synonymous with the repression of individuality.

The more creative corporations were quick to adopt a whole new language to appeal to the new currents. Board members and CEOs would talk about autonomy, creativity, empowerment, liberation, and networks. Anti-work slogans had been washed away from the city walls only to reappear in corporations' annual reports.

At the beginning of the 1970s, business gurus in the United States had started to make the same realizations. Many young people, especially those who felt a strong desire to express their authenticity, looked at corporations with suspicion. For executives, this presented a serious problem. They knew that, while this younger generation might pose challenges to the corporations in the short term, they also presented invaluable opportunities in the long run. If they could attract these young creatives on board, they had much to gain. In 1970, two articles appeared in *Harvard Business Review*, each of which set out to make this claim. The first of them, written by Joe Kelly, talked about the 'turbulent times', and the challenges that this posed for corporations. The second text, entitled 'An Anatomy of Activism for Executives', written by Samuel A. Culbert and James M. Elden, went much further. They discussed, up front, the US invasion of Cambodia and the ensuing student protests at UCLA and Kent State University, the latter resulting in the National Guard shooting and killing four students.

Each of these texts announced that it was time to stop sweeping conflicts under the carpet, and instead use them in a productive manner. 'Old concepts of human relations, including the notion that conflict per se is harmful and should be avoided at all cost, do not square with the facts any longer,' Kelly wrote. 'Indeed, the new approach is that conflict, if properly handled, can lead to more effective and appropriate arrangements.'[21] Angry young people had to be engaged in dialogue, because, in a few years' time, they would enter corporations as colleagues of the older generation. But more importantly, management needed new insights and ideas, and that is precisely what this younger generation possessed. This is the key point that Culbert and Elden set out. 'If executives could only open their eyes to what underlies slogans like "revolution" and "liberation", they could profit from, rather than merely react against, the motivation of educated youth.'[22]

It is fascinating to read these words now, almost fifty years after they were first written. Today, we can see how numerous companies have followed this advice and successfully brought the slogans of revolution and liberation into their corporate culture. But when we look closer at these workplaces, we see that the slogans can also be used to extend working hours and to blur the line between life and work.

## The Hidden Costs of Authenticity

The critique against the 9-to-5 work rule continued long after the Beats and the hippies. But when Dolly Parton released her hit '9 to 5' in 1980, the traditional form of 9-to-5 work life was already beginning to fade. Ronald Reagan was about to take office, and his UK counterpart, Margaret Thatcher, had already been in office for more than a year. Together with Thatcher, Reagan was about to spearhead a neoliberal revolution. To this end, he used a daring political strategy. While appealing to 'inner directed' people, who, despite occasionally holding left-leaning sentiments, found that the expression of individuality was more pressing than social inequality, he could easily go ahead and roll back government, pushing more and more people into an incredibly vulnerable position. In 1981, after 13,000 air-traffic controllers went on strike to demand better work conditions, Reagan responded fiercely, firing nearly all of them. During his time in office, Reagan also tried to lower the minimum wage for young people and encouraged federal agencies to employ temporary workers.

Politicians of all stripes followed suit, legitimizing their initiatives under the euphemism of 'market labour flexibility'. Soon, millions of people were thrown into the precariat, where, instead of holding long-term, stable, fixed-hour jobs, they had to rely on occasional jobs, short-term contracts, fluctuating hours, unpredictable salaries, and few career prospects.[23]

What market labour flexibility actually means, Guy Standing argues in his book *The Precariat*, is that 'risks and insecurity' are transferred 'onto workers and their families', culminating in 'the creation of a global "precariat"', consisting of millions around the world 'without an anchor of stability'.[24]

Having no stable income over extended periods, constantly moving from one short-term contract to the next, replacing one gig with another, the precariat lives, Standing argues, with constant anxiety – 'chronic insecurity associated not only with teetering on the edge, knowing that one mistake or one piece of bad luck could tip the balance between modest dignity and being a bag lady'.[25]

The technological innovations of the last couple of decades have allowed many people to work at all places, and at all times. As management gurus say goodbye to work–life balance and instead welcome what they call work–life integration, unproductive pockets of life are increasingly under threat. In *24/7: Capitalism and the Ends of Sleep*,[26] Jonathan Crary argues that capitalism now seeks to colonize people at all times, including when they sleep. In the United States, he claims, the average person has gone from sleeping ten hours at the beginning of the twentieth century, to eight hours in the 1950s, to six and a half hours today. As Crary argues, we are now expected to be switched on at all hours, without interruption. According to this logic, sleep becomes a form of barrier to 24/7 capitalism. But now also sleep is threatened with subordination to the logic of productivity.

It is no news that, in many professions, the line between life and work has largely disappeared. What is perhaps more noteworthy, and worrying, is that some workers are unable to ever switch off, resulting in them being productive even when asleep. A few years ago, an IT worker wrote a moving essay about being unable to ever disengage. He was not simply dreaming *about* work, as many people do, but he found himself actually working, solving problems in his sleep. The tragedy, he explained, was that he could no longer envision anything outside of work, except on the rare occasion of getting ill.[27] This might be more common than we previously thought. According to a recent survey on mobile workers, 38 per cent of the respondents said they woke up at some point during the night to check their emails.

This is the condition of what Byung-Chul Han calls an 'achievement society', which 'is slowly developing into a doping society'.[28] When every moment is translated into an opportunity to make yourself more productive or more effective, then there are no longer any pockets of unproductive time, outside of capitalist accumulation. This obsession with achievement and activeness 'is generating excessive tiredness and exhaustion'. Worse, it is a solitary tiredness. It has, Han continues, 'a separating and isolating effect'.[29]

We have come full circle. The tiredness and exhaustion that Bukowksi experienced in his daily work has reappeared. This time, however, the exhaustion does not come from work, but from our investments in work. Bukowski saw this was coming when, as quoted in the epigraph above, he 'learned that it wasn't enough to just do your job, you had to have an interest in it, even a passion for it'.

More than complying with one's contract, employees are now urged to think of work as an opportunity for discovering their true spirit. But when work is transformed into an abstract pursuit of happiness, employees are left wondering where to draw the line.

## The Violence of Precarity

In 1930, the British philosopher Bertrand Russell observed that work can be more or less exciting, ranging 'from mere relief of tedium up to the profoundest delights'.[30] While work is generally dull, it has the advantage of relieving people from the existential burden of making active choices. When we are engaged in work, we don't have to worry about how to best spend our free time. In short, work is a 'preventive of boredom'.[31]

Today, however, work is rarely described as an escape from boredom. Instead it has become an obligatory path to happiness. At a place like Zappos, happiness is not a fortunate side-effect of the work the company does, but the essence of its philosophy. Happiness is what it delivers to its customers, in the form of a shoe box. And it is what it delivers to the employees, once they have invested themselves emotionally in the company. It wants the employees to connect and engage with their work. They should not be there because they have to, but because they really want to – because they 'love it'.

Russell claimed that meaningful and constructive work, which allows people to exercise a particular skill, can be a source of great satisfaction. In 2015, close to 50 per cent of American workers said they were satisfied with their jobs. While this was an increase over the last ten years, it still left half of the population dissatisfied. The difference between the 1930s, when Russell contemplated the possibility of conquering happiness through work, and the time of emotional capitalism that we live through today is perhaps not that there are infinitely more 'interesting' and 'stimulating' jobs available now, but simply that workers are expected to be happy in their jobs, regardless of how poor and detrimental the circumstances may be. As Miya Tokumitsu notes in *Do What You Love*, 'Projections of work-as-love have also seeped into the realm of low-wage service work.' As an example, she notes that 'a maid-service company advertising on Craiglist is currently looking for a "passionate individual" to clean houses'.[32] In an essay in *London Review of Books*, Paul Myerscough explains that workers at Pret a Manger, the UK fast-food chain, are not just required to look happy and positive. They have to *be* happy. As one Pret manager put it: 'The authenticity of being happy is important.'[33] The fact that the starting salary is just above the UK minimum wage is, of course, beside the point.

In a workplace like Zappos, where employees supposedly 'love their jobs' and work–life balance has been replaced by work–life integration, there is no longer any need to worry about those 'castration shears' that Raoul Vaneigem warned against, because the two blades, work and leisure, have properly morphed into one. But when nothing seems to exists beyond work, 'doing what you love' can easily turn into a nightmare. As a study from 2015 reveals, while many office workers report being happy with their jobs, they nevertheless feel burnt out. As Tokomitsu notes: 'Mantras like "Do what you love" and "Follow your bliss" frequently cloak a ruthless ideology of nonstop production and consumption in the cozy comfort of self-care and pleasure.'[34] When happiness is no longer a possibility, but a necessity, employees need not only to report on their happiness, but also to express their happiness in a sincere manner. 'Luckily for employers,' Tokomitsu continues, 'the popular culture of insistent happiness codified by DWYL [do-what-you-love] provides an efficient way for workers to outwardly and insistently project how thrilled they are to be working.'[35]

As the line between work and non-work has vanished, and more and more people are expected to pursue happiness through work, we can see the emergence of what Byung-Chul Han calls a burnout society.[36] After a century of steady decline of working hours – from 3,000 in 1870, to 1,887 in 1973 – this trend came to an abrupt end. From 1973 to 2006, the average American worker had added 180 more hours to their annual working schedule, while wages have remained largely flat.[37]

While overwork has become normalized in many places, some corporations have taken it one step further to boast about it. 'You can work long, hard or smart, but at Amazon. com you can't choose two out of three,' the CEO Jeff Bezos wrote in a letter to his shareholders. A *New York Times* report revealed the inhumane work culture at Amazon. One of its former marketers, who had since left the company, explained that his 'enduring image was watching people weep in the office'.[38]

Even though Amazon acquired Zappos in 2009, it has not made happiness its crucial message. While there are great differences between these companies' cultures, we can see how Amazon also draws inspiration from the 1970s version of the human potential movement, as it was taking on a more corporate shape. Among its key 'rules' we find a familiar one, namely that 'Employees are to exhibit "ownership" (No. 2), or mastery of every element of their businesses, and "dive deep".'[39]

'Taking ownership over your own life', as the phrase was originally devised in the early days at Esalen, has now become a commonly used slogan in many corporations. In the *New York Times* report, Amazon is described as 'harsher and less forgiving' than most other corporations; it considers harmony to be 'overvalued' and fosters an atmosphere of 'honest critique'. According to rule no. 13, Amazonians should 'disagree and commit', which means they should 'rip into colleagues' ideas, with feedback that can be blunt to the point of painful, before lining up behind a decision'.

This is a modern version of Perls's hot seat, where all employees have to come forward and confront their fears and engage in honest self-critique. They need to share their thoughts and ideas without censoring themselves. But there is one crucial difference. The workers at Amazon are not engaging in these activities to free themselves from any authority figures and find their true inner selves. They engage in these activities to demonstrate their performance. They are constantly monitored and evaluated, and those at the bottom are thrown out of the company. As one employee said, 'it is in everyone's interest to outperform everyone else'.[40] This is where the logic of capitalist fundamentalism meets the techniques of the human potential movement.

As the Italian philosopher Franco 'Bifo' Berardi remarks, in an era of capitalist absolutism, all 'of our collective energies are enlisted to one goal: to fight against all others in order to survive'.[41]

At Amazon, colleagues made 'quiet pacts' to 'bury the same person at once'. One former employee had received constantly high ratings for years. Then her father unexpectedly got ill and she had to spend time to take care of him. Soon after, she was informed that she had become 'a problem'. Like all others who didn't reach the performance targets, she was laid off. This was 'purposeful Darwinism', as a former human resource executive described it. This philosophy is not far from Werner Erhard's notion that there are no victims. At Amazon, those who 'suffered from cancer, miscarriages and other personal crises' were quickly 'edged out'.[42] This is the logical conclusion of Erhard's notion that we are responsible for everything that happens in our lives, whether we are mugged on the street, hit by a car, sent off to a concentration camp or contract cancer.

Bifo argues that when everyone competes with one another, a new type of mind-set emerges. Workers feel alone, 'facing the blackmail of merit, the humiliation of failure, the threat of being made redundant'. Social relations break down. Everyone feels guilty. They blame one another for the 'mutual inability to help each other, to build solidarity'.[43]

This is what the happiness fantasy has turned into today. Work is not standing in opposition to happiness, as it did for the Beat generation. Nor is it an avenue towards happiness, as Russell had it. No, happiness is an obligation that workers need to express and experience, even in places and situations where happiness seems to be remote. The happiness fantasy is not the workers' fantasy of a richer and more interesting work life; it is the manager's fantasy of being able to do what they want with their employees. It is a fantasy that is best summed up in Trump's slogan: 'You're fired!'

As I will argue in the next chapter, we can see a similarly strange transformation in relation to drugs. If, in the Sixties, drugs were commonly used as a way of escaping the flat and boring world of institutions and professional demands, they are now repackaged as a means to become more productive and more creative – in short, better adapted to the world of work.

4

# Getting High on Happiness

To fathom hell or soar angelic.
Just take a pinch of psychedelic.

Humphrey Osmond

## Tune In, Turn On, Drop Out

In a 1966 interview with CBC, Leonard Cohen explained that, in his view, happiness and drugs are by no means incompatible. 'Everything keeps on going, or it stops,' he begins, somewhat elusively, in his dark, characteristic voice. 'I mean, you know when you're happy. There's been so much talk about the mechanics of happiness: psychiatry, and pills, and positive thinking, and ideology. But I really think that the mechanism is there, all you have to do is get quiet for a moment or two and you know where you are.'[1]

'And for this knowing where you are,' the interviewer

asked, 'you don't need the help of anything like drugs or liquor or anything?'

'Well, it's not a matter of the help,' Cohen responded, 'but you can co-operate with the vision that alcohol gives you; you can co-operate with the vision that LSD gives you. All those things are just matter of plants, and they are there for us, and I think we ought to use them.'

Almost three decades earlier, in 1938, while working at the Sandoz Pharmaceutical Laboratory in Switzerland, the chemist Albert Hofmann was having an unexpected break-through. He was creating alkaloid-like compounds which were thought to have medically positive effects on the uterus, and the twenty-fifth compound – named LSD-25 – did indeed have 'strong uterine-constricting effects'.[2]

The compound was set aside. Five years later, in 1943, Hofmann decided to go back and synthesize it again. By accident he ingested an infinitesimal amount. Still, it was enough to make him feel slight, strange effects. The follow-ing week, he decided to make a controlled self-experiment, using what he believed was 'a ridiculously safe amount of the substance: 250 micrograms'. This time, the feeling was more than just slight, and he 'became "strangely inebriated", the shape of time became distorted, and fantastic colors and shapes began to appear before his eyes'.[3] Hoffman had discovered a dangerously powerful molecule. He had had the world's first LSD trip.

A few years later, at the beginning of the 1950s, the CIA became interested in the drug. The rumour was that the Soviet Union had stocked up massive quantities of LSD, with the intention of using it in warfare.[4] While the rumour turned out to be false, it had nevertheless made the CIA interested in exploring the possible uses of the drug, and so they began financing a series of research experiments across American universities.

Meanwhile, in 1953, the novelist Aldous Huxley had befriended the psychiatrist Humphrey Osmond, who, at the time, was working at a Canadian mental hospital, exploring the possible use of mescaline in the treatment of schizophrenia.[5] Before they first met, Huxley and Osmond had started corresponding with each other, and it was in an exchange between the two that the word 'psychedelic', as specifically referring to mind-altering drugs, was first coined. 'To make this trivial world sublime. Take half a gramme of phanerothyme,' Huxley wrote. And Osmond responded: 'To fathom hell or soar angelic. Just take a pinch of psychedelic.'[6]

Soon after, in May of that year, Osmond travelled to California to see Huxley. He had brought a dose of mescaline with him, which Huxley, under the supervision of his wife and Osmond, then ingested. Huxley recorded the drug-infused eight-hour trip that followed. When under the influence, during a walk in the garden, he noted that 'my body seemed to have dissociated itself almost completely from my mind'. 'It was odd,' he continued, 'to feel that "I" was not the same as these arms and legs "out there", as this wholly objective trunk and neck and even head.' As he was looking around the garden, Huxley was struck by its beauty. A chair suddenly became the object of intense fascination: 'Where the shadows fell on the canvas upholstery, stripes of a deep but glowing indigo alternated with stripes of an incandescence so intensely bright that it was hard to believe that they could be made of anything but blue fire.'[7] Huxley's observations and experiences, along with a more philosophical and historical meditation on the subject of mescaline, resulted in his 1954 book *The Doors of Perception*, which was soon going to attain cult status among the growing bands of countercultural bohemians, especially those with an interest in psychedelics. It even inspired the name of the rock band The Doors.

LSD was perfectly suitable for the culture of the time. As Carl Elliott observes: '[P]sychedelic drugs, like sex and communal living, were seen as expressions not merely of hedonism, but also of a desire to get in touch with more authentic ways of living.'[8]

Unsurprisingly, Esalen, with its promise to deliver authenticity, was at the centre of the psychedelic movement. Already from the start, visitors to Esalen could attend courses involving 'mind-opening drugs'. One of the first seminars to be delivered in 1962 was called 'Drug-Induced Mysticism'. The course was kept on the programme for the following years and became one of the institute's most popular. Included in the reading list were Huxley's *The Doors of Perception* and *The Joyous Cosmology*, which recounted Alan Watts's own experiences with LSD.

Watts, who had been at Esalen since the start, had initially been reluctant to test LSD. He had not been convinced by the enthusiasm that the Beat authors had expressed for marijuana, peyote, and other mind-altering substances. He didn't think they were 'portals to religious experience'.[9] But when Watts finally tried LSD, prompted by Huxley himself, he found the experience so profound he decided to write a book on the topic.

In *The Joyous Cosmology*, published in 1962, Watts begins by levelling a fierce critique against the insistence among many philosophers to separate mind from body, claiming that this duality has 'changed man from a self-controlling to a self-frustrating organism'.[10] Eastern mysticism, by contrast, refuses the separation between the material and the spiritual, and Watts wished to bring that realization to Western culture. One avenue for doing so was through the use of psychedelic substances, and he experimented with LSD, mescaline, and psilocybin to this end. When taking the substances, he could sense how the boundaries between mind and matter disappeared: '[T]he world is at once inside my head and outside it.'[11] Like Huxley, he experienced a new sense of perception, and was careful to point out that what he saw was not hallucinatory, but simply another way of seeing things. 'The landscape I am watching,' he observed during one of his trips, 'is also a state of myself, of the neurons in my head. I feel the rock in my hand in terms of my own fingers. And nothing is stranger than my own body – the sensation of the pulse, the eye seen through a magnifying glass in the mirror, the shock of realizing that oneself is something in the external world.'[12]

Like Leonard Cohen, who suggested that LSD could co-operate with happiness, Watts argued that while 'these drugs do not impart wisdom', they 'provide the raw material of wisdom'. They may help to realize the true nature of joy.

Timothy Leary and Richard Alpert, two iconic figures who preached the gospel of LSD and its positive effects, endorsed Watts's book, calling it 'the best statement on the subject of space-age mysticism'.[13] In their preface, Leary and Alpert described it as a potent critique of 'the politics of the nervous system', a kind of politics which 'involves the mind against the brain, the tyrannical verbal brain disassociating itself from the organism and world of which it is a part, censoring, alerting, evaluating'. They claimed that the politics of the nervous system was a mind-controlling apparatus. Its function was to regulate and censor the way people think and behave. And LSD, they thought, was an instrument that could be used against such a system. It could bring about a distinct sense of freedom – 'freedom from the learned, cultural mind'. 'The freedom to expand one's consciousness beyond artifactual cultural knowledge. The freedom to move from constant preoccupation with the verbal games – the social games, the game of self – to the joyous unity of what exists beyond.'[14]

In the early 1960s, as two young psychologists at the Harvard Center for Research in Personality, Leary and Alpert had devised a series of experiments with psychedelic drugs, especially psilocybin, a synthetic form of mescaline. Both Leary and Alpert were later dismissed from the university, and started their own organization, the International Foundation for Internal Freedom. 'I left Harvard in 1963,' Leary later wrote, 'abandoned the role of conventional, academic, scientist, and became, without knowing it, a shaman, and an activist change-agent.'[15] Both Leary and Alpert became prominent figures in the Sixties countercultures, and Leary became widely regarded as the leader of the psychedelic movement.

Leary had come to believe – as did many others with him – that psychedelic drugs were not just a way of exploring new dimensions of the self and its intimate relation to the material world, as had been proposed by Huxley. There was also a social and political dimension, Leary claimed, and LSD could be used as a weapon against an oppressive world. As such, psychedelic substances were not just a chemical issue; they were a political one too. They promised a revolution. As Walter Truett Anderson puts it in his 1983 book *The Upstart Spring*, there was a belief that 'psychedelic drugs would bring the transcendental religious experience within reach of everybody, overthrow the old consciousness that is the source of all oppression, and swiftly change the world.'[16]

Leary was open about his intellectual debt to Huxley, naming *The Doors of Perception* as a great source of inspiration. Hoping to gain his support, Leary went to see him in 1962. But Huxley was not impressed. In a letter to Osmond, Huxley wrote of Leary: 'He talked such nonsense.'[17]

Yet Huxley's reservations would have little effect on Leary's popularity. As Adam Smith puts it in his 1975 book *The Powers of Mind*, 'Leary thought he was on the edge of a revolution.'[18] Whether the revolution ever happened or not, Leary was at the forefront, and in 1967 made an historic appearance at Golden Gate Park, where he spoke to tens of thousands of people. They had gathered for a massive peaceful protest, prompted by a new Californian law banning LSD. In his speech, Leary delivered an unforgettable catchphrase, which came to be synonymous with the movement. 'Tune in, turn on, drop out,' he declared. Although it was Marshall McLuhan who had first coined the phrase, he was happy for Leary to use it. For Leary, drugs were not simply about getting high and travelling one's inner cosmos. They could be used as part of the larger aspiration to drop out of society: 'I mean,' he said in his speech, 'drop out of high school, drop out of college, drop out of graduate school.'

From its accidental emergence in a Swiss laboratory in the early 1940s, LSD had become a central symbol for a generation that wanted not just to alter their old self-frustrating minds, but to overthrow the old world. The drug became a symbol for the revolution they dreamt of, a life of authentic happiness – beyond the social control exercised by institutions, beyond paternal authority figures, and beyond self-censoring, repression, and renunciation. It was the fantasy of happiness, based on Reich's dream of natural and sexual happiness, although brought about in the form of a substance, a substance that was designed to kill 'the little man', overcome the punishing superego, and set the individual free.

But as we will see, there were not only libertarian renegades such as Leary who preached the transformational powers of drugs. At around the same time, pharmaceutical companies and psychiatrists began launching campaigns in which they championed the use of chemicals in the pursuit of happiness – or in the war against unhappiness.

## The Case Against Medicines

Like Huxley, the Hungarian-born psychiatrist Thomas Szasz was not impressed with Timothy Leary. A few years before his death, in *Coercion as Cure*, Szasz described Leary as a 'lapsed Catholic, defrocked psychologist', who 'preached a narcissistic, nihilistic and pathetic message, addressed to the young faced with the task of growing up and joining the world of responsible adulthood'.[19]

Even though Szasz believed that adults should be free to use drugs if they were so inclined, he did not, like Leary, see in them the potential to bring about a revolution. Moreover, Szasz subscribed to an entirely different notion of what it meant to be human, and did not ascribe the same potential to chemicals as did Leary, who thought that the human mind had to be liberated from society's conventions, and that chemicals could be usefully employed to this end. Indeed, Leary believed that 'man did not know how to use his head, that the static, repetitive normal mind was itself the source of "dis-ease" and that the task was to discover the neuro-chemical for changing mind', and that 'LSD might be such a drug'.[20]

For Szasz, however, the problem was not that people were trapped inside their 'normal mind' and needed to be liberated through the use of LSD. He was worried that the medical sciences would pathologize the normal mind. Whether psychedelics or sedatives, Szasz did not see the liberating potential of such medications.

In 1963, the same year that Leary was dismissed from Harvard, Szasz coined the term 'therapeutic state'. The phrase was meant to denote what he saw as 'the political union of medicine and state', where physicians were 'playing the same sorts of ambiguous, double roles that priests played when church and state were united'.[21] Szasz was only one among an emerging band of critics, sometimes lazily and unhelpfully referred to as anti-psychiatrists, who tried to draw attention to the socio-political side of psychiatry.[22] Even though organized resistance against psychiatry existed already in the late nineteenth century, it was not until the 1950s, with the advent of antipsychotic drugs, that the theory and practice of psychiatry became subjected to critical scrutiny.

While the CIA funded LSD experiments at universities, hoping to learn more about that drug's potential use for controlling the mind, critics such as Szasz were busy articulating their unease with what they saw as the rise of a repressive society, one that was drawing on the discourse of psychiatry and medicine to deepen and widen its reach. In 1961, Szasz published his first seminal work, *The Myth of Mental Illness*, which claimed that psychiatry was nothing but a pseudoscience, best compared with astrology or alchemy.[23] Mental illness, he went on to claim, was not an illness at all, but a mere myth produced by psychiatrists in a hope to gain control over human behaviour. As he would later put it: 'As there is no egg in eggplant, there is no illness in mental illness.'[24]

A few years earlier, the Dutch psychiatrist Joost Meerloo had expressed similar concerns. In his 1956 jeremiad *The Rape of the Mind*, Meerloo cautioned against the new medicines that had now entered the market, and advised his colleagues not to adopt them too blindly. Although Meerloo did not name any particular medicines, it is likely that he referred to the new controversial antipsychotics that were launched at around this time. As a practising psychiatrist, he had observed the emergence of a propaganda campaign. 'My desk overflows with gadgets and multicolored pills telling me that without them mankind cannot be happy.'[25] Meerloo warned his colleagues against prescribing 'sedatives and stimulants' in those cases where they, as physicians, should rather have been seeking the 'deeper causes of the difficulties'. Meerloo was worried that the triumph of the therapeutic had entailed a rather naïve belief according to which all people, however serious their ailments, could quickly and easily be restored to a state of happiness. What he most worried about was that doctors, like himself, would stop searching for the root cause of patients' suffering, and instead take the easy way out and prescribe drugs. Such an instrumental orientation to human behaviour, Meerloo argued, could have devastating effects on the individual's liberty and independence. He saw the emergence of an invasive politics, aiming to 'bring the human mind into submission and servility'. As he put it, somewhat bluntly: 'Drugs and their psychological equivalents are also able to enslave people.'[26]

Interestingly, this propaganda campaign was drawing on the same vocabulary as the psychedelic movement did. Leary referred to himself as a shaman and an activist change-agent. Through the use of drugs, he had become capable of seeing through the mores of society. It had helped him realize that happiness was not to be sought through bourgeois norms. It was not to be achieved by becoming part of stable institutions, whether the family, school, or work. Rather it was to be gained by opting out – that is, by disconnecting oneself from all oppressive agents of organized society and set oneself free.

For Meerloo, however, this was an illusion – the same illusion that the drug-mongering establishment of therapy was now exploiting. It was actively using the 'fiction that we have to use miracle drugs in order to become free-acting agents'.[27] But instead of making people free, Meerloo argued, these drugs would just turn them into dependent people. 'Drugs and medical techniques can be used to make man a submissive and conforming being,'[28] he claimed, also noting, in a somewhat conspiratorial manner, that 'chemical dependents are weak people who can be made use of by any tyrannical political potentate'.[29]

What we see here are two conflicting theories of the relation between drugs and happiness. On the one hand, we have Leary, for whom drugs have the potential to produce a new sense of happiness, based on authenticity and enjoyment. On the other, we have Szasz, for whom drugs prevent any form of authentic happiness. For him, this chemical notion of happiness was both narcissistic and nihilistic.

Szasz was indeed critical of institutional powers and their grip over individuals. But he did not see any revolutionary power in the use of pharmaceuticals or psychiatric treatment. Rather than setting people free, and making them capable of better connecting with their emotions, people under the influence of medicine were prone to abuse. They were likely to be caught in a psychiatric machine, which would make them not more free, but more docile and compliant. The sort of happiness that medications brought was not a happiness of authenticity, but one of inauthenticity. Once on the drugs, people had lost something of themselves. They had become dependent, not independent.

In various shapes and forms, this critique continued to be levelled against the psychiatric establishment in the following decades. The image of the medicated individual was an image of loss. It was of someone who was no longer him- or herself. Perhaps the most striking (and lasting) image of the medicalized patient was produced in Ken Kesey's 1962 novel *One Flew Over the Cuckoo's Nest*. He describes the scene of patients sat in the day room, all of them immersed in their own peculiar activity, as simultaneously sad and amusing'. 'Like a cartoon world,' Kesey writes, 'where the figures are flat and outlined in black, jerking through some kind of goofy story that might be real funny if it weren't for the cartoon figures being real guys...'[30] But then, as a speaker-voice informs them it is time for medication, they line up, receive a paper cup with their medication, swallow the pills, and are no longer real – yet perfectly docile and controllable.

### Prozac and the Promise of Authenticity

And then, in 1987, came Prozac. Like the medications prescribed to the patients in Ken Kesey's dystopia, Prozac had a profound effect. But instead of smoothing out the edges, and making the person more docile and conformist, Prozac had the opposite effect: making them feel real. At least this was the effect according to some of its users.

In his 1993 bestseller *Listening to Prozac*, Peter Kramer noted how one of his patients, Tess, reacted in a surprisingly positive manner to Prozac. She suddenly felt as if she had come alive. She had not lost her sense of self, but finally obtained it. 'I am myself again,' she had told Kramer, 'I am myself again.'[31] For the first time in her life, she started dating men. She didn't just like the attention, but also enjoyed the complex game of courting. 'I had never seen a patient's social life reshaped so rapidly and dramatically,'[32] Kramer wrote.

She then tried to get off the medication. It worked for a while. Then she slipped. She contacted Kramer again, telling him: 'I'm not myself.'[33]

Kramer was puzzled: first, when on medication, Tess felt real; and then, without it, she felt unreal. Although he was uncertain if she was depressed at the time, he could no doubt see how she was on the wrong track, and so went ahead and prescribed the medication again. And, luckily, it did work. Once again, she was back to her new self.

Prozac had been a popular medication since it was launched in 1987. But it was not until now, when Kramer talked to Tess, that he understood the real reason for its success: it made people feel authentic.[34]

While he was happy for Tess, Kramer also felt uneasy. What had happened to all of those intimate traits that Tess had previously associated with her sense of self? Had they just been erased? Was her entire past narrative false, as if someone had mixed up the tapes when she was born?

As Kramer put it: 'Suddenly those intimate and consistent traits are not-me, they are alien, they are defect, they are illness – so that a certain habit of mind and body that links a person to his relatives and ancestors from generation to generation is now "other".'[35] Prozac had given Tess a new sense of who she was. She had been able to construct a fresh self-narrative and started to evaluate issues of health and pathology in an entirely different manner. She had, Kramer claimed, 'located a self that feels true, normal, and whole', and saw medication as 'an occasionally necessary adjunct to the maintenance of that self'.[36]

What is striking with this case is that Tess did not just 'improve' or 'enhance' herself. More dramatically, she had altered her experience about who she was. She had found her *real* self.

In *Better Than Well: American Medicine Meets the American Dream*, American philosopher Carl Elliott convincingly argues that, in an era where authenticity is experienced as a moral calling, all sorts of self-enhancement technologies, including medication, take on a new meaning. Rather than being fake, they allow the individual to be real:

This, as much as anything, helps to explain the pull of the language of authenticity of enhancement technologies. It is a way of justifying them to yourself, countering the imagined criticism that they represent a kind of phoniness, narcissism, or status-seeking. No, they are none of these, you say; it was only when I got the face-lift, started on steroids, got a sex-change operation, that I really felt like myself.[37]

Such was also the experience that the iconic actor Cary Grant had when first testing LSD as part of a scientific experiment. It had completely changed him, Carl Elliott recounts, adding that LSD helped him peel 'away all of the vanities and hypocrisies and playacting that his social role had encouraged him to develop and perform'. On LSD Grant could for the first time 'peek into the inner chamber' and 'discover who he really was'.[38]

But, of course, not all people are so lucky as to discover themselves through drugs, whether LSD or Prozac. In *Is It Me or My Meds? Living with Antidepressants*, David A. Karp retells an array of stories from people with experiences from depression and the use of drugs. One of the people Karp interviewed struggled with his identity: 'I don't feel like the same person on drugs. I feel as though maybe I'm a better person, but it's not who I am.' A woman in her early sixties explained how her therapists had told her that the pills would make her more herself, but how, instead, she felt as if 'the pills take me away from me, they do something else'. Another woman about the same age described a similar experience. Under the influence of the drugs, 'I couldn't think. I couldn't even drive. I wasn't me. And that's a horrible feeling.'[39]

Not everyone experienced the same sense of self-discovery as Tess did. Many experienced a sense of loss instead, feeling as if their real selves had gone astray. Although the patients' stories differ, however, they have one thing in common, and that is their insistence on evaluating the drugs in relation to their sense of self, and whether or not the drugs help them experience a sense of authentic selfhood. Perhaps these stories say less about medicine and psychiatry than they say about the difficulties of feeling authentic.

According to the happiness fantasy, one cannot be happy unless one has first discovered one's true inner self. Psychiatric discourse and pharmaceuticals are by no means detached from society's norms and values. Our experience of medication and therapy is hugely influenced by cultural currents. But as we will see now, psychiatry is not simply mirroring the happiness fantasy, but is also instrumental in shaping the fantasy of what it means to be a happy and healthy human being.

## The Pathology of Happiness

In a paper from 1992, published in *Journal of Medical Ethics*, the clinical psychologist Richard P. Bentall proposed that happiness should be classified as a psychiatric diagnosis and included in the *DSM* (*Diagnostic and Statistical Manual of Mental Disorders*). Issued by the American Psychiatric Association, the *DSM* is the standard manual used by psychiatrists to keep track of the ever-increasing list of diagnoses, informally known as the 'Bible of psychiatry'.[40] Bentall argued (ironically, of course) that happiness is 'statistically abnormal, consists of a discrete cluster of symptoms, is associated with a range of cognitive abnormalities, and probably reflects the abnormal functioning of the central nervous system'.[41] It is a disease that reflects a 'lack of contact with reality'. Bentall recommended using the technical term 'Major Affective Disorder, Pleasant Type', to ascertain 'scientific precision' and reduce 'any possible diagnostic ambiguities'.[42]

When the 132-page volume of the *DSM* was published in 1952, it was surrounded by controversies. A psychological study had been published three years earlier revealing that psychiatrists were incapable of using the same criteria when determining the diagnosis of a patient. Even when they were presented with the exact same information about a patient, they only agreed on 20 per cent of the cases. A few years later, in 1962, a follow-up study showed that psychiatrists were still more likely to disagree than agree.[43]

Despite its lofty scientific aspirations, seeking to catalogue and define all conceivable forms of mental illnesses, the *DSM* was nevertheless a product of its time, shaped by the prevailing values of the era. A well-known example is that homosexuality was listed as a psychiatric diagnosis up until 1973. And even then, it lived on for a few more years under the term 'Ego-Dystonic Homosexuality', which referred to those who were gay, not by choice, but involuntarily, and for that in need of therapeutic support. As Greenberg observed: 'It was a win-win: gay people would no longer be subject to bizarre and pointless therapies (or to psychiatrist-assisted discrimination), the APA would stop getting humiliated by protest, and therapists everywhere would continue to get insurance dollars to treat gay patients.'[44]

Over the years, the *DSM* has grown in size: from 134 pages in the second revision published in 1968, to 500 pages in *DSM-III* launched in 1980, to 886 pages in *DSM-IV* published in 1994.

The most recent revision, *DSM-5*, published in 2013, comes in at just under 1,000 pages. While I have no desire to throw myself into an already infected debate, it is worth nothing that this latest revision of the manual is not only larger in size and more comprehensive than the previous revisions, it is also more inclusive. It has adopted a so-called 'preventive approach', which means that early signs of a disorder may be enough to classify as a diagnosis. If a child throws more than three tantrums a week, it may be enough to earn the diagnosis 'Disruptive Mood Dysregulation Disorder'. If you eat more than you should on two or more occasion in one week's time, then you may suffer from 'Binge Eating Disorder'. If you forget the name and face of people, feel muddled or occasionally over-exalted, then you may be diagnosed with one of the following diagnoses: 'Minor Neurocognitive Disorder', 'Mixed Anxiety/ Depressive Disorder', or, possibly, 'Adult Attention Deficit Disorder'.

How could we explain this explosion of diagnoses? While psychiatrists are no doubt at the centre of this trend, they are not solely responsible. Pharmaceutical companies play an active role, too. For instance, to get a new psychotropic drug approved by the Food and Drug Administration (another central actor in the politics of pharmaceuticals), they often need to connect it to a particular diagnosis. And this means, in somewhat simplified terms, that the more inclusive a diagnosis is, the more people it will encompass – which, by extension, implies more sales of the medication.

In *White Coat, Black Hat*, Carl Elliott takes us on a

harrowing journey through the dark corners of the medical industry, revealing, among many other things, how medical corporations are marketing their medicines in cunning ways. For instance, some pharmaceutical companies have hired ghost-writers to write and publish 'scientific articles' in which they present results that tend to be favourably disposed to the medicine, either exaggerating its benefits or overshadowing its side-effects. One medical communications company, called Current Medical Directions, was paid by the pharmaceutical giant Pfizer to produce a series of research papers on the antidepressant Zoloft. In an independent investigation led by David Healy and Dinah Cattell, it was revealed that Current Medical Directions, during the period they were paid by Pfizer, had published more articles about Zoloft than all other independent researchers had done together. And unsurprisingly, the articles produced by Current Medical Directions presented Zoloft in a more favourable light than those that were independently researched.[45] This is just one of the strategies used by corporations to push the sales of their drugs.

However, 11 per cent of all Americans aged twelve and above are now using antidepressants, and this cannot alone be explained by cunning marketing strategies. 'To blame the drug industry for prescribed-drug addiction,' Ivan Illich wrote in his 1975 book *Medical Nemesis*, is like 'blaming the Mafia for the use of illicit drugs.'[46] To understand the popularity of drugs, we need to consider their usefulness in relation to the demands that people face. In our present-day ideology, based on relentless competition, people are expected to work hard to brand themselves, network, connect, and search for opportunities. Ingrained as they are, these demands are difficult to simply ignore. They are also hard to live up to, as the compulsory narcissists will testify to. Shocking or not, pharmaceuticals can be incredibly useful for people who are otherwise struggling to live up to the expectations placed on them, whether to engage socially or concentrate on work.

As Elliott describes in *Better Than Well*, even though the purpose of many medications is to help people deal with various social demands they face, this is something that medical companies have to be careful not to say too loud. In the late 1960s, the pharmaceutical company Sandoz launched a marketing campaign for Serentil, a medicine that would help anxious people fit in. 'For the anxiety that comes from not fitting in', the slogan read, promising to help anxious people become better at dealing with bosses, friends, and relatives. This campaign was later banned. According to Elliott, the advertisement revealed, all too explicitly, that the medicine was designed not exclusively to cure a medical condition, but also to help people deal with social pressures.[47]

Attaining the happiness fantasy today is not easy. It presupposes an ability to be authentic as a human being; to enjoy life to the fullest; and to be successful at branding oneself and making it on the market. These values are not only demanding in themselves, but can also be contradictory when pursued simultaneously. It is no wonder, then, that some people turn to drugs in their pursuit to become more effective and to achieve professional success.

## The Conformity of Smart Drugs

For Timothy Leary, LSD was more than just a spiritual experience. It helped him discover a new way of life and liberate himself from the bourgeois conventions of his childhood. With the help of LSD, he could detach himself from the demands that had been imposed from school, work, and family. Better still, on LSD he never had to grow up. He did not have to work. He could turn on and tune in. He could drop out. He could just *be*.

In 2015 a reporter at *Vice* magazine tried modafinil, a drug that was synthesized in France in the 1970s, and approved by the FDA in 1998 for treatment of narcolepsy.[48]

Like other users, he had taken the drug to give his ability to concentrate 'a kick up the ass'. The first thing he noticed was that he didn't feel like smoking. Instead he was 'hungry for work' and agreed to take on extra tasks. Dutifully, and with no apparent appetite, he ate his lunch pizza and then, instead of going out for a walk or having an after-lunch cigarette, as he would normally do, he returned to his desk and continued working. When his boss came over to his office in the afternoon, he was impressed by his achievement. He carried on working, feeling irritated by his colleagues, who interrupted his productivity. 'The casual desk chat that I usually enjoy and promote suddenly seemed offensive,' he explained, 'not against me, but, even worse, against my work.' All of the things he would normally enjoy – going for a walk, watching a comedy show, smoking a joint – now seemed like a waste of time. As he summarized his experience:

> Modafinil may be the least fun drug there is (at least of the ones
> I've tried), but in the rat race that is modern life, it's sort of the
> only one that makes sense. It's weird, isn't it? The same young
> people who enthusiastically welcomed love drugs like MDMA
> and pills are now into taking things like modafinil – which,
> ironically, only makes you love work.

Modafinil and other drugs used to improve concentration for longer periods have become hugely popular in
American colleges. Some surveys indicate that as many
as one in seven students have used these medications to
perform better.[49]

These students don't seem to subscribe to Leary's advice
to 'drop out'. Rather, they use illicit drugs to deal with
mounting demands and pressures. Chemicals are used
not to explore the mind, but to connect with particular
tasks. These are not the drugs of the narcissist who gives
the finger to the establishment and opts out. They are the
drugs of the compulsory narcissists, who ingest chemicals
to opt in. They are used to become more productive, more
competitive.

Perhaps it is unfair to compare hallucinogenics such as
LSD with psychoactive stimulants such as modafinil, but the
point here does not concern the drugs themselves, but how
they are made meaningful in relation to a specific cultural
milieu. While modafinil became important in relation to a
discourse of productivity and competition, LSD attained its
meaning in relation to Leary's fantasy of opting out.

But as it happens, more recently, people have experimented with LSD in the pursuit of becoming more

productive. In a 2015 article in *Rolling Stone* we meet 'Ken', a twenty-five-year-old graduate from Stanford, now working for a San Francisco start-up, who ingests small doses of LSD to enhance his creativity and productivity. As the article states, 'regular doses of acid have become the creativity enhancer of choice for some professionals'.[50]

The ideals of authenticity and hedonism, as they emerged together in the countercultures of the Sixties as an attempt to break free from the chains of society, have now morphed into something else. When college students use performance-enhancing drugs to get themselves through long and tiresome hours in the library, or start-up entrepreneurs engage in micro-dosing to enhance their creativity, they are doing it neither in an attempt to express their true individuality, nor as an avenue to enjoyment.

And yet this is the language that is employed by corporations and the medical establishment today. We are told that work and business ventures are routes for individuals to express themselves. And we are led to believe that the discourse of employability allows individuals to discover their hidden talents and make them visible to the world.

But we all know that these are neoliberal euphemisms, devised to normalize precarious life. And it seems as if the same applies to the use of psychotropic drugs. They are used not in the pursuit to discover one's authentic self, but as a means of getting a competitive advantage, making oneself more productive and hopefully more successful. We seem here to be very far away from the promise of hedonism and the life of pleasure.

What happens with our ability to gain pleasure in a culture that is arranged not only around work and competitiveness, but also around the notion that we should use every moment to pursue bodily and spiritual satisfaction?

# 5

## Pleasuring Men

There is no pleasure I haven't actually made myself sick on.

Philip Seymour Hoffman

### All-Inclusive Pleasure

'This is paradise,' my mother said as she sat down on the sunbed next to the swimming pool with a gin and tonic in a plastic glass. She squinted against the sun, enjoying the warmth. It was late October in Gran Canaria and we had left behind a cold and grey Sweden earlier that morning. My daughter was playing in the pool with her cousins. I followed the life-guard in his white T-shirt and red shorts as he moved across the pool area, picking up trays with empty glasses on them. It was late afternoon and the guests were retreating to their hotel apartments to change for dinner. The temperature was reaching 32 degrees Celsius.

It had been a tough autumn for me. Too much work. I

was looking forward to a week of relaxation. My hope was to lie in the sun reading books, listening to the sea as it rolled in. But even though the sea was just a stone's throw away, I never heard the sound of the waves from where I lay. Instead I heard loud house music streaming from the speakers behind me. Twenty people were doing mysterious movements with rubber bands, mimicking the buff man in sleeveless shirt standing in front of them. A few minutes later, a young woman walked to the edge of the pool with a microphone: 'In five minutes, the pool games will start. Doesn't matter if you're old or young, join me in the biggest pool splash ever!'

I headed into the restaurant, got myself a beer, and retreated to my sunbed.

Each year, between 3 and 4 million people come to Gran Canaria for a holiday. Exhausted by work and depressing weather, they arrive there, bleak and weak, hoping to return one week later tanned and refreshed. Like my family, many of the visitors have no intention of travelling the island and exploring the culture. All they want is to stay by the pool and slowly get tipsy from the free drinks, feeling the kind of happiness that comes from pleasure. While hardworking travel guides entertain the children with various games, the adults are left alone to do whatever they want, whether yoga, scuba diving, tennis, or, as I preferred, nothing at all.

By the end of the week, as I sat with my family in one of the restaurants eating a Nutella pizza, I could not help thinking this must be the most concentrated form of pre-packaged hedonism there is. Everything was available. Entertainment from morning to late evening. Restaurants offering a huge selection of food. Bars with beer and wine and cocktails. And all the while, the sun was overhead, shining relentlessly.

This was the happiness fantasy, based on unrestrained hedonism. Prior to the rise of the consumer society, something like this could only have taken place in small private circles, such as the infamous dinners hosted by the emperor Caligula, where the guests were offered an abundance of exotic food and entertained with live sex performed by slaves. But now, these excesses have been made available for millions of Westerners who wish to take a break from their ordinary lives, and enjoy themselves for a week.

### Killing Pleasure

In December 2012, just over a year before his tragic and premature death, Philip Seymour Hoffman appeared on the stage of the Rubin Museum of Art to discuss happiness with the philosopher Simon Critchley.[1] 'I have thought a lot about this, actually, in my life lately,' Hoffman said at the start of the conversation, 'and gotten nowhere with it.' To lend the discussion a deeper theoretical level – to be, as Critchley put it, 'professorial for a moment' – the philosophy professor began by presenting one distinct philosophical model of happiness as a starting point: 'One way of thinking about happiness is that happiness is a pleasure, and there's a kind of wish I have for …' – Critchley peeks at his take-away latte, sitting next to him on the side-table – '… coffee. And I get coffee, and that gives me pleasure and that makes me happy.' Hoffman ponders the question for a while, then states, 'I would definitely say that pleasure is not happiness. I kill pleasure. ... I take too much of it ... too much coffee and you're miserable. ... There is no pleasure I haven't actually made myself sick on.'

These words have a chilling resonance. On 2 February 2014, Hoffman was found dead in his home. He had a syringe in his left arm, and the police found nearly fifty envelopes of heroin in his apartment.[2] But when Hoffman, in the discussion about happiness, said that he kills pleasure, he did not simply talk about his own personal problems. Rather, he was putting his finger on a peculiar aspect of enjoyment, about which psychoanalysts have reminded us of for a long time: the enjoyment we hope to achieve is never going to be as good and fulfilled as the enjoyment we eventually get. This I had learnt first-hand from spending a whole week in an all-inclusive resort drinking copious amounts of gin and tonic. After a few days of relentless enjoyment, I was beginning to feel exhausted and my throat was sore.

But what Critchley had in mind, in his 'professorial moment', was not the kind of hedonistic excess offered at all-inclusive resorts or through the illegal substances that Hoffman might have referred to. What he had in mind was the Epicurean doctrine that pleasure is 'the root of all good' and, as such, 'the beginning and the end of the happy life'.[3] Epicurus is often referred to today as the Greek philosopher who praised the pleasurable life. Yet while it is true that he saw pleasure as the route to happiness, his theory is often misunderstood. The notion of pleasure and hedonism that he promoted is very far from what we associate with enjoyment today.

Epicurus was born on the Greek island of Samos in 341 BCE. Like an early beatnik, he spent much of his adolescent years on the road, roaming around Greece taking up various jobs, working for a while as a soldier then a schoolteacher, before finally, in 306 BCE, settling down in Athens, where he set up his own school, called the Garden. From the descriptions that have survived, the school seemed like a pleasant place to be, with a long table placed in the garden and people eating and discussing philosophy for hours on end.[4] As such, he lived according to the same philosophical principles that he preached. He masterfully shied away from all forms of practical responsibilities, not participating more than necessary in the social and political life of Athens, spending as much time as possible with his close friends at the Garden, studying, writing, thinking, and discussing. To Epicurus, the simple pleasures were also the most sublime ones. He loved food and drink, but kept a simple and restrained diet, avoiding both meat and wine.

Google 'hedonism' and browse through the images and you will see pictures of half-naked young people dancing on beaches or shirtless macho men binge-eating deep-fried chicken. It is fascinating to note that, to Epicurus, this form of indulgence had nothing to do with hedonism. For him, pleasure as a way of life meant avoiding all kinds of excess. Sex and intoxication, let alone binge-eating, were for him deviations from the true path to happiness. As he put it in a Letter to Menoeceus: '[W]hen I say that pleasure is the goal of living I do not mean the pleasures of libertines or the pleasures inherent in positive enjoyment.'[5]

Seeking pleasures like a libertine was futile, Epicurus claimed, hence echoing the same argument that psychoanalysts would later make: that attaching too great hopes in what pleasure could bring, one would inevitably end up disappointed. Worse, one would be imprisoned in a circular and destructive pursuit of pleasure. A much better strategy, Epicurus thought, was to stick to the simple pleasures, because what one gained from pursuing simple pleasure was freedom. The best one could achieve as a human being was to live without fears and come to terms with the most precious wisdom of being alive, namely that what is good and pleasant is easy to achieve and what is bad and painful is easy to endure.[6]

This is an optimistic notion of life, and I have to admit feeling drawn to it, occasionally thinking I should try to live more like an Epicurean, cutting down on drinking and eating more vegetables. But I would argue that this vision might underestimate the paradoxical nature of pleasure. Epicurus explains that the desires we should pursue are those that are natural and necessary, because the pleasure we get from eating food comes not from the taste, but from the elementary function of appeasing hunger.

Cruising around an all-inclusive resort with a drink in my left hand and a pizza slice in the other, I could appreciate what Epicurus had in mind. In today's consumer society, we are trained to pursue pleasure through consuming all forms of products, not just those you can eat, but anything you can buy. It is no wonder then that people want to escape this world of non-stop enjoyment, whether by moving out to the countryside to live a simple self-sufficient life or by going off to remote places on detox retreats.

But in the days of Epicurus there were not many open-all-night supermarkets. 'We consider limitation of the appetites a major good,' he says, 'for the purpose of enjoying those few in case we do not have much.'[7] Today, if you feel like a snack in the evening, it should not be too hard to find one. And there is nothing luxurious about chocolate bars or soda or even beer. In most places, these items are cheaper than fresh vegetables. What people with limited financial resources are worried about today is not the supply of tasty snacks. They are worried about more fundamental necessities, such as being able to pay the rent or cover the electricity bill.

When Philip Seymour Hoffmann said that 'there is no pleasure I haven't actually made myself sick on', he seemed to touch both on the universal question of enjoyment, as an inherently paradoxical quest, and on the way our consumer society bombards us with the message that we need to enjoy. Like many others, myself included, Hoffman was never able to find happiness through pleasure. He was far from mastering the Epicurean art of regulating his life according to his natural pleasure. His autopsy found traces not just of heroin, but also of cocaine, benzodiazepines, and amphetamines.

## A Brief Case Study of Manly Despair

It was that perfect time of the day, just before dinner, and it was beginning to cool down a little. I was sitting with my wife on the terrace of our hotel apartment, drinking a glass of cava.

'The only thing that isn't available on tap here is sex,' I said. 'Maybe there are places like these but for swinger couples.'

'Have to be,' she said 'But maybe not with swingers, but with prostitutes.'

Which was when I started thinking of Michel Houellebecq, the French author, who has written a couple of books about tourism, one of which was even set on an island close to where I was now, in Lanzarote. But the book I had in mind was *Platform*, from 2001, where we follow the protagonist Michel as he goes to Thailand for sex tourism but falls in love with a woman who works in the holiday industry. When they return again to France, they devise a new strategy for saving the tourist company she works for. The plan is to merge the classic holiday-club model with sex tourism. The name and slogan: 'Eldorador Aphrodite: Because pleasure is a right.'[8]

I should probably emphasize that I don't read Houellebecq from the perspective of a literary critic. I read him as a social and cultural critic. As an academic with an interest in popular culture, I am often reminded that it is not only academics who are engaged in producing social science. To my mind, some of the finest analyses of our society are made by novelists, journalists, and filmmakers – what the sociologist Roger Burrows calls 'social science fiction'.[9]

What makes Houellebecq interesting for the following discussion is his ability to critically diagnose a society based on the imperative to enjoy. He takes the moral values we endorse in today's consumer culture, such as the right to accumulate wealth and the right to pleasure, and then reveals the tragic underside of these values. The world we encounter in Houellebecq's works is ruthless and hopeless, and his anti-heroes have adapted themselves to this world by accepting this ruthlessness and giving up all hope, except the hope of occasionally appeasing their sexual desires. As he puts it in his 1994 novel *Whatever*: 'In a totally liberal economic system certain people accumulate considerable fortunes; others stagnate in unemployment and misery. In a totally liberal sexual system certain people have a varied and exciting erotic life; others are reduced to masturbation and solitude.'[10] When reading Houellebecq, we don't see much of those with exciting erotic lives. Instead we meet the failures who are reduced to masturbation and solitude. Unattractive and with low self-esteem, they are losers in the 'liberal sexual system'. But they are able to rectify this situation, at least to some degree, because they are, as white middle-aged men with decent incomes, winners in the 'liberal economic system'.

Such is the situation for Bruno, the anti-hero of *Atomised*, from 1998, whose entire life has been occupied with sex. Already as a teenager he had been rejected by the girls he knew, and when we meet him, at the age of forty-two, we are informed that his erections have become 'shorter and more infrequent' and that he feels 'himself succumb to a sad decline'.[11]

I will dwell on this book for a little while because I can think of no other text better at describing the transformation of the happiness fantasy, from its optimistic character in the 1960s as a vision of an alternative world, to what it has become today, when fully absorbed in a culture defined by competition. The question we encounter here is: what are the possibilities of pursuing happiness through sexual pleasure in the twenty-first century if you are considered both unattractive and uninteresting?

Bruno is one of two brothers born in the second half of the 1950s to Janine, a freewheeling hippie mother. Since Janine was more interested in the *experience* of giving birth than actually being a mother, she found it perfectly sensible to leave Bruno and his younger half-brother Michel in the custody of their respective grandparents. Janine, liberated from the drudgery of motherhood, could continue her cosmic adventures. She travelled to California and changed her name to Jane.

*Atomised* is a book about growing up in the shadow of the happiness fantasy. Bruno and Michel's mother has lived her life according to the twin ideals of authenticity and sexual pleasure, as they were promoted by Wilhelm Reich and Fritz Perls, and she has been handsomely rewarded for this quest. She has lived an adventurous life with a steady stream of young lovers. From a distance, she appears to be happy.

For her sons, however, the reality is grim. In their futile quests to become happy, they have set out on different paths. Michel has searched for and to some degree found happiness in the abstract world of bioscience, a world that is far away from the tyranny of other people. Bruno, on the other hand, has found nothing. 'His only goal in life had been sexual,' Houellebecq writes, 'and he realized it was too late to change that now.'[12] In his early forties, he can look back on a difficult childhood and a 'ghastly' adolescence. The future looks equally bleak. Even though his entire world has been organized around sexual love, his experiences have been scarce, limited to prostitutes and women he did not really find attractive. Even so, sex has made him feel good regardless, and that is all that matters. It is the only thing that could make him happy.

'Could a canary be happy?' Houellebecq asks in his usual dead-pan manner in the opening pages of the book, before delivering his own specific definition of the term. 'Happiness is an intense, all-consuming feeling of joyous fulfilment akin to inebriation, rapture or ecstasy.'[13] It is the kind of happiness that a canary would probably not be capable of. But is Bruno? Maybe. At one point in the book, while having sex, he describes how his whole body 'shuddered' with happiness.[14] Sadly, that only happened once and it was a short-lived experience.

Bruno has embraced the moral values of the happiness fantasy. He has made, as Freud put it, 'genital eroticism the central point of his life'.[15] In an aspiration to pass himself off as authentic and cool, he grows a goatee and buys a leather jacket.

The tragedy of Bruno's quest for sexual happiness reaches its apogee when he decides to go to a fictional version of the Esalen Institute, called Lieu, in Western France. The institute was opened in 1975 by a group of

'68 veterans who wanted to create an 'authentic utopia'. In the 1980s, as it was running into financial difficulties, they began offering a series of courses in personal development and positive thinking, aimed at business people. Soon, they had attracted many of the largest and most reputable companies, including IBM. While the target group was now human resources directors, the Lieu still retained its 'reputation as a hedonist's paradise, which became its unique selling point'.[16]

The other participants seem happy. They are 'living, breathing, striving for pleasure or trying to develop their personal potential'.[17] Bruno is hoping to get into the same mode. He even signs up to a range of courses, including 'Sensitive Gestalt-Massage', which is an eroticized version of Fritz Perls's Gestalt therapy. But engaging in these activities doesn't make him sexually and spiritually liberated. It only strengthens his sense of depression. Night after night, he ends up alone, in his own tent, drinking whisky, masturbating to a porn magazine which has written, on the front page, the ironic slogan 'pleasure is a right'.[18]

For Houellebecq, the sexual revolution was not a communal utopia. It was 'simply another stage in the historical rise of individualism'.[19] Bruno is not equipped to deal with that world. Embracing the happiness fantasy, as it is embodied by his mother, only reminds him of his failure. He is neither able to find sexual partners who desire him, nor able to restyle himself as a cool authentic person. Finally, he realizes 'there's no point in trying to pass myself off as a dropout. I'm not young or good-looking enough and I'm certainly not cool enough.'[20]

## The Alpha Male's Right to Pleasure

On 7 October 2017, less than two weeks after *Playboy* founder Hugh Hefner died at age ninety-one, Hollywood producer Harvey Weinstein issued a statement against numerous allegations of sexual assault that had been published in the *New York Times* a couple of days earlier: 'I came of age in the '60s and '70s when all the rules about behavior and workplaces were different. That was the culture then. I have since learned it's not an excuse, in the office – or out of it.' Oliver Stone and Woody Allen came to Weinstein's rescue, which did little to convince the public of his innocence. Only the fact that they felt a need to speak out, journalist Wesley Morris writes in a *New York Times* article, 'illustrates an enduring, but misguided, myth of the sexual revolution. We romanticized Mr Hefner's empire as a revolutionary force – lovers gonna love, and all of that – but it was actually just a popularization of entitlement.'[21]

When Hefner launched the first issue of *Playboy* in 1953, featuring a nude photo of Marilyn Monroe, the times were still culturally conservative. But the mood was changing rapidly and the magazine struck a chord and became a success over night. As Matt Schudel wrote in his obituary of Hefner, the 'magazine was shocking at the time, but it quickly found a large and receptive audience and was a principal force behind the sexual revolution of the 1960s'.[22]

More than half a decade later, when Hefner's death was announced, he was no longer seen as a revolutionary of the Sixties. In his silk pyjamas and bathrobe, he was the image of patriarchy and abuse, an old man compulsively surrounding himself with young half-nude women. As Ross Douthat put it in his unflattering obituary, Hefner 'was a pornographer and chauvinist who got rich on masturbation, consumerism and the exploitation of women, aged into a leering grotesque in a captain's hat, and died a pack rat in a decaying manse where porn blared during his pathetic orgies'.[23]

And yet, Hefner's legacy lives on. Just consider Berlusconi and Trump. Or Trumpusconi, as Frank Bruni has put it in a *New York Times* essay, arguing they are 'essentially the same man'.[24] To make this point, readers were invited to take a quiz, guessing who of the two men had said what. 'Last night I had a queue outside the door of the bedroom' (Berlusconi). 'My fingers are long and beautiful, as, it has been documented, are various other parts of my body' (Trump). 'I think the only difference between me and the other candidates is that I'm more honest and my women are more beautiful' (Berlusconi). 'When asked if they would like to have sex with me, 30 percent of women said, "Yes," while the other 70 percent replied, "What, again"' (Berlusconi).

The right to pleasure, as it was promoted by Wilhelm Reich and Fritz Perls, finds in the image of Hefner and Trumpusconi its logical conclusion. As the happiness fantasy begins to crumble, we can see that the right to pleasure has nothing to do with people's right to explore their sexuality. For instance, neither Trump nor Berlusconi regards homosexuality favourably, to put it diplomatically. No, the right to pleasure is a right to which only the rich and powerful are entitled, best expressed in the slogan: you can do what you want to do and get away with it.

These are men beyond self-critique, radiating an unbounded sense of narcissism. In a perceptive essay in the *Los Angeles Review of Books*, the historian Elizabeth Lunbeck claims that Trump's narcissism is not a liability but a resource. He has successfully branded himself as a person who can do whatever he wants without having to apologize. What he offers people is participation in his greatness. If we wish to understand Trump, we should stop asking whether he is a narcissist or not, and start considering how he exploits 'his narcissism to connect with his followers'.[25]

The happiness fantasy, as it brings together the notions of being oneself (without worrying too much about others), pursuing enjoyment (in the form of sleeping with women), and becoming successful through one's career (achieving positions of power), is a distinctly male fantasy. It is based on entitlement, self-mastery, and selfish accumulation. It is a fantasy that fetishizes the image of the self-made man, and his ability to become great, at the expense of others.

This right to happiness as pleasure can be traced all the way back to Reich and his 'phallic' theory of happiness. For Reich, the only way to become happy and fulfilled as a human being was to develop one's orgastic potency. When he first launched this theory in the 1920s, some of his psychoanalytic colleagues started referring to him as a 'genital narcissist', a term which did not offend Reich, because he was sure that this was nothing more than an expression of their 'sexual jealousy' and the fact that 'they weren't as "potent" as he'. Like Trumpusconi, Reich often boasted about his own orgastic potency, as when he at the age of fifteen had been with a prostitute and experienced a theological union with the phallus, describing the experience in his diary: 'I was all penis.'[26]

This genital happiness fantasy inspired Fritz Perls to develop Gestalt therapy, a method that aimed to liberate a person, both spiritually and sexually. When Perls took residence at Esalen at the age of seventy, he became known as the 'pasha of the hotsprings'. According to Turner, 'he would successfully seduce women with such memorable lines as "You want to suck my cock?"'[27] Like Reich and Trumpusconi, Perls saw himself as an alpha male. He referred to himself as a polymorphous pervert, and was proud to be known both as a dirty man and a guru, even though, as he put it, 'the first is on the wane and the second ascending'.[28]

Unlike the characters we find in Houellebecq's novels, these are the alpha males who have benefited greatly from the happiness fantasy, using it as an excuse to 'be themselves' (assholes), pursue pleasure (with or without consent), and blend their persona with the brand. If this is what the happiness fantasy has become, it is about time to let it go, and let the Trumpusconis go down with it.

# Conclusion

## *Happiness After Trump*

If I had been the son of a coal miner, I would have left the damn mines.

Donald Trump

### Trump's Happiness Fantasy

The first episode of *The Apprentice*, which aired on NBC on 8 January 2004, opens with a set of striking images of New York from above. 'Manhattan is a tough place,' Donald Trump says in a voice-over as the camera cuts from skyscrapers to a homeless man sleeping on a bench. 'If you're not careful, it can chew you up and spit you out.' Another cut, now to a big mansion. 'But if you work hard, you can really hit it big – and I mean really big.' One more cut. Trump sits in the back of a limousine, staring into the camera, introducing himself as the city's largest real estate developer.

The imagery speaks for itself. As Naomi Klein writes in her book on Trump and his 'shock politics': '[Y]ou can be the homeless guy, or you can be Trump.'[1] In his version of the American Dream, there were winners and there were losers – and Trump was a winner. He was the ultimate expression of success – a person who had achieved the happiness fantasy. He had come to this place through hard work, a determination to never give up, and an ability to use his imagination. In 1990, in an interview with *Playboy* magazine, Trump said he liked to tell the story of the coal miner's son: 'The coal miner gets black lung disease, his son gets it, then his son. But most people don't have the imagination – or whatever – to leave the mine. They don't have "it." If I had been the son of a coal miner, I would have left the damn mines.'[2] Branding himself as a self-made man, Trump rarely mentions the $40 million he inherited in 1974,[3] let alone the connections he made through his father when he started working in the family business after graduating from college. To Trump, these were purely incidental circumstances, largely irrelevant in explaining his own success. Had he been the son of a coal miner, he would have used his imagination to leave the mines. He would have ended up in a limousine regardless.

The term 'the American Dream' was coined by the popular historian James Truslow Adams in *The Epic of America,* published in 1931. He defined it as 'a dream of a social order in which each man and each woman shall be able to attain to the fullest stature of which they are innately capable, and be recognized by others for what they are, regardless of the fortuitous circumstances of birth or position'.[4]

But to understand Trump's version of the American Dream, we should turn not to Adams, but to the American minister and motivational speaker Norman Vincent Peale, who was a close friend of Trump's family, even officiating Trump's wedding with Ivana in 1977.

In his 1952 classic bestseller *The Power of Positive Thinking*, Peale presents a simple and 'workable philosophy' to help people live happier and more successful lives. The technique is simple: 'prayerize, visualize, actualize'.[5] By using this technique, you can achieve anything – overcome defeat and take control over the circumstances of your life.

Like Trump, Peale had a habit of telling people anecdotes, invariably casting himself in the role as hero. We hear about a woman who was able to bring back her husband by visualizing him at home; a recovering alcoholic whom Peale telepathically saves from a relapse; and a man who fixes his toe by asking the Lord to send it 'right back to the plant'.[6] For Peale, these stories illustrate a profound truth, namely that attitudes are more important than facts. This insight, Peale continues, 'is worth repeating until its truth grips you'.[7]

Surely, this 'truth' had gripped Werner Erhard when he said that there were no victims in the world. It was the same kind of 'truth' that prompted Oprah Winfrey to congratulate people who had been laid off. It was this 'truth' that emboldened the UK television presenter Noel Edmonds to suggest, in a tweet, that cancer is caused by a bad attitude.[8] And it is also this truth that we find at the core of the happiness fantasy.

It is not easy to capture the cruelty underlying this 'truth', but there's a remarkable scene in the 2008 documentary *Three Miles North of Molkom* that comes close. The film follows a group of people attending a New Age festival in Sweden. They entertain themselves with yoga, tantric sex, tree hugging, and fire walking. They also learn a little-known martial art called yellow bamboo. The idea of this technique is simple. You use psychic energy to defend yourself.

The group stand on a beach, led by an instructor. 'Breathe in and pull the energy down,' he says. 'And push it out of your hands.' Then we see a woman. She steps into place. She gathers as much psychic energy as she can, pulling the energy down from the air, into her body, and then out through her hands. The close-up reveals her nervousness. She looks insecure, fragile. The instructor comes running forward at a fast speed. Something is not right. *Bang!* She falls to the ground, crying.

In case it wasn't obvious: shooting out invisible arrows of psychic energy from your hands is not going to help you when a full-grown man attacks you. And the same goes for a positive attitude. A positive attitude won't be enough to help the homeless man off the street and into Trump's limousine. It won't be enough to help a long-term unemployed person to get a well-paid job. And it won't cure cancer. Saying that attitudes are more important than facts is delusional, which a group of Australian researchers were able to confirm.[9] They asked 179 cancer patients to complete questionnaires assessing their optimism. When the patients later died, the researchers could see whether there was a connection between their optimism and the duration of their survival. There wasn't.

Trump's happiness fantasy is used not to inspire common people to pursue their dreams, but to normalize exploitation and gross inequalities. Trump's world is a jungle of dog-eats-dog capitalism. 'Week after week,' Naomi Klein wrote about Trump's show *The Apprentice*, he 'delivered the central sales pitch of free-market theory, telling viewers that by unleashing your most selfish and ruthless side, you are actually a hero – creating jobs and fuelling growth. Don't be nice, be a killer. That's how you help the economy and, more importantly, yourself.'[10]

When Reich's happiness fantasy spread to large groups of young people in the 1960s it was a fantasy of creating a society free from constraints, abuse, and domination. Even though the reality was less rosy than the fantasy, there was still an element of hope. More than half a decade later, it is hard to see the remains of that hope. When embodied by Trump, the happiness fantasy with its insistence on authenticity and pleasure no longer looks that appealing. Who wants to be authentic when it means being selfish, ruthless, and not listening to others? Who believes in the right to pleasure when it is used by Weinstein and Trumpusconi to take advantage of women? And how can we believe that work is the route to an authentic life filled with pleasures when we see how low-wage workers are forced to smile authentically to make it look as though they really enjoy their work?

From Freud and Reich, via Aldous Huxley, Alan Watts, and Timothy Leary, to Werner Erhard, Tony Hsieh, and

Donald Trump, the happiness fantasy has, from beginning to end, been expressed and defended by men. In the course of researching this book, I was frustrated by constantly running into men, and was actively looking for female voices to balance the account. But then I gave up, thinking it might be better and more honest to let the men speak. After all, this was their fantasy, serving their interests. Sure, the happiness fantasy in the Sixties was more inclusive. Voices that had previously been silenced were now included. But female voices were nonetheless suppressed and manipulated. As Jenny Diski reminds us in her book *The Sixties*, as sex was no longer a taboo, it was uncool for women to say no. 'It was difficult to come up with a justification for refusing to have sex with someone that didn't seem selfish.'[11]

So, even in this period, the happiness fantasy was phallic in character. It was a fantasy of self-mastery, authenticity, and the right to pleasure, which many men exploited to get laid. Right from the start, it had been a fantasy of prestige and status. And later on, in the 1970s and 1980s, it became a fantasy of gaining and exploiting one's power and wealth.

As we begin to call into question the basic values underlying this notion of happiness, we soon realize we don't have to live this way. Happiness fantasies are constructed. They are assemblages of the moral values that happen to be esteemed at a particular time. What we regard as a happy life now, in the rich West, is something entirely different from how it was envisaged and pursued in ancient Greece or the Middle Ages. It is also different from how happiness is construed in other parts of the world, although the

American version of the happiness fantasy has travelled far beyond its national borders, to influence people like myself who have lived most of their lives in the cold North, watching American television and listening to American music.

Though constructed, these fantasies have an almost magical ability to appear natural and inevitable, as in the 1960s and 1970s, when the fantasy of self-actualization and pleasure became seen not just as moral ideals but as moral demands. In other periods, as when Reich first promoted his notion of sexual happiness, most people looked at this fantasy with suspicion. If fantasies of the good life go through periods of stability and periods of instability, I would argue that we are now at a point where our current happiness fantasy is beginning to fall apart. While the richest 0.1 per cent are rewarded with more tax cuts, a large portion of the American working and middle classes struggle to get by. For them, and for many others, this happiness fantasy has lost its attraction.

And this is good news, because it means we can now begin to imagine new fantasies, beyond the phallic fantasies of authenticity, hedonism, and self-mastery.

## A Feminist Happiness Fantasy?

Unlike food critics, who get free dinners, feminist writers get free death threats, Laurie Penny writes in *The Bitch Doctrine*. She explains that, as a female writer, she is often told that her anger is not about politics but about her inability to get laid. 'I have empirically tested this hypothesis, and I still have a list of demands,' Penny observes wryly. 'Top of that list is a kinder world.'[12]

Perhaps this is not a bad place to start when imagining a new happiness fantasy, although it might be naïve to ascribe too much importance to a word that has become popular with both corporations and politicians – recalling, for example, George W. Bush's ludicrous term 'compassionate capitalism'. But even so, in the current climate of hatred and cruelty, we could certainly do with a bit more kindness.

One step in this direction is to stop thinking of happiness as a personal pursuit. Instead of a happiness fantasy based on the notion that we should win ourselves and become authentic, we could perhaps imagine a happiness fantasy in which we lose ourselves and become inauthentic. We would lose ourselves in the sense of acknowledging our fundamental dependency on others, including people we will never get to meet or know. In *Precarious Life*, the philosopher Judith Butler makes a strong case for imagining a community based on 'vulnerability and loss', arguing that loss has a transformative effect which can prompt people to come together as a 'we'.[13]

Loss and vulnerability abound in today's world, whether we think of refugees embarking on hazardous travels in the hope of finding a safer place to live, or poor British families struggling to cover their electricity bills, or indebted graduates in the United States working for free in the hope of finding a stable job. Different as they are, these experiences of precariousness could perhaps form the basis of a shared notion of what it means to live together in a spirit of inter-dependence and solidarity.

Such a happiness fantasy would be premised on empathy rather than selfishness. It would be inclusive rather than exclusive, empathizing with the vulnerable, such as the woman in agony on the beach after being floored in the yellow bamboo exercise, or the unemployed or the cancer patient.

It would be a fantasy that begins not with the individual's dream of self-realization, but with a collective demand for a more compassionate, equal, and truthful world. Aldous Huxley once said that 'there is something curiously boring about someone else's happiness'.[14] I was reminded of these words recently when reading Lynne Segal's book *Radical Happiness*: 'As a feminist,' she writes, 'I have always taken the pleasures and joys of others seriously.'[15]

Even though Huxley, unlike Trump, considered human differences to be a great resource for society, he nonethe-less promoted a very individualistic notion of happiness. What Segal presents in her book is something much more appealing. Instead of the personal happiness fantasy we find in self-help manuals, she presents a political and col-lective happiness fantasy based on a shared experience of joy. She argues, with Cornel West, that joy can cut across the individualistic notion of happiness. It can take us out-side of our immediate everyday experiences and direct us towards more profound values, such as love, kindness, and solidarity.

A feminist happiness fantasy would take both the hap-piness and the vulnerabilities of others seriously. And while hopeful about the future, it would not shy away from uncomfortable truths related to the state of the planet, the state of human rights, and the state of justice.

Guided by such a fantasy, we would no longer be impressed by people – mainly men – who boast about their personal transformation and quest for authenticity. We would not reward those – mainly men – who selfishly pursue their own personal goals at the expense of others. We would no longer tolerate sexual violations – committed, almost exclusively, by men – in the name of a right to pleasure. And together – women *and* men – we would imagine new ways of living and working, which are not defined by market values alone.

Does this sound naïve? Of course it does. But who cares? As Laurie Penny puts it: 'In case you hadn't noticed, there's a war going on. The field of battle is the human imagination.'[16] All I wish to say here, as my last words, is that I would rather invest myself emotionally in an impossible fantasy I can believe in than hold on to a fantasy that has proved, again and again, to be only cruel and delusional.

# Notes

## Introduction

1 Jeffrey J. Kripal, *Esalen: America and the Religion of No Religion* (Chicago: University of Chicago Press, 2007).

2 Jenny Diski, *The Sixties* (London: Profile Books, 2010), p. 9.

3 Diski, *The Sixties*, p. 5.

4 Darrin M. McMahon, *Happiness: A History* (New York: Atlantic Monthly Press, 2006).

5 Daniel Bell, *The Cultural Contradictions of Capitalism* (New York: Basic Books, 1976).

6 Mark Fisher, *Capitalist Realism: Is There No Alternative?* (London: Zero Books, 2009), p. 22, emphasis in original.

7 Paul Myerscough, 'Short Cuts', *London Review of Books* 35(1), 3 January 2013.

8 Joan Didion, *Slouching Towards Bethlehem* (New York: Farrar, Straus and Giroux, 1968).

9 This story is partly inspired by the third episode of Adam Curtis's documentary *The Century of the Self*, in which he looks at Wilhelm Reich and his influence on the human potential movement and, by extension, at Werner Erhard. While there are some similarities in the narrative between Curtis's documentary and this book, my approach is altogether different. Whereas Curtis focuses on

consumerism and marketing, I focus on happiness and how it has become integrated into the culture of work and helped shape a particular version of neoliberal subjectivity, based on precariousness.

## Chapter 1  In Bed with Wilhelm Reich

1  Wilhelm Reich, *Listen, Little Man!* (New York: Farrar, Strauss and Giroux, 1945/1974), p. 26.
2  Philip Rieff, *The Triumph of the Therapeutic: Uses of Faith After Freud* (Chicago: University of Chicago Press, 1966/1987), p. 155.
3  Jack Kerouac, *The Dharma Bums* (New York: Viking Press, 1958), pp. 73–4.
4  Reich, *Listen, Little Man!*, p. 7, original emphasis.
5  Jackson Lears, *Fables of Abundance: A Cultural History of Advertising in America* (New York: Basic Books, 1994), p. 189.
6  Alexis de Tocqueville, *Democracy in America* (New York: Doubleday, 1835–40/1969), ch. 34, p. 516,
7  Christopher Turner, *Adventures in the Orgasmatron: How the Sexual Revolution Came to America* (New York: Farrar, Strauss and Giroux, 2011), p. 113.
8  Reich, *Listen, Little Man!*, p. 27.
9  Reich, *Listen, Little Man!*, p. 29.
10  Reich, *Listen, Little Man!*, p. 43, original emphasis.
11  In telling the story about Reich I have drawn on a large number of sources, especially his own written work and his diaries and letters. Even so, I need to mention Christopher Turner's wonderfully rich and entertaining biography of Reich, *Adventures in the Orgasmatron*, on which I draw freely and heavily throughout this chapter.
12  Wilhelm Reich, *Passion of Youth: An Autobiography, 1897–1922* (New York: Farrar, Strauss and Giroux, 1988), p. 81.
13  Sharaf R. Myron, *Fury on Earth: A Biography of Wilhelm Reich* (New York: St Martin's Press, 1983), p. 54.
14  Myron, *Fury on Earth*, p. 57.

15  Myron, *Fury on Earth*, p. 57,
16  Wilhelm Reich, *The Function of the Orgasm* (New York: Pocket Books, 1927/1975), pp. 5–6.
17  Sigmund Freud, 'Civilization and Its Discontents', *The Standard Edition of the Complete Psychological Works of Sigmund Freud, Volume XXI, 1927–1931* (London: Vintage, 2001), p. 83.
18  Mary Higgins and Chester M. Raphael, eds, *Reich Speaks of Freud: Wilhelm Reich Discusses His Work and His Relationship with Freud.* (New York: Farrar, Straus and Giroux, 1967), p. 5.
19  Higgins and Chester, eds, *Reich Speaks of Freud*, p. 6.
20  Higgins and Chester, eds, *Reich Speaks of Freud*, p. 20.
21  Reich, *Passion of Youth*, p. 6.
22  Turner, *Adventures in the Orgasmatron*, p. 41.
23  Walter Benjamin, *One Way Street and Other Writings* (New York: Penguin, 2009), p. 9.
24  Myron, *Fury on Earth*, p. 58.
25  Turner, *Adventures in the Orgasmatron*, p. 52.
26  Turner, *Adventures in the Orgasmatron*, p. 57.
27  Turner, *Adventures in the Orgasmatron*, p. 54.
28  Turner, *Adventures in the Orgasmatron*, p. 52.
29  Wilhelm Reich, 'The Impulsive Character', *Journal of Orgonomy* 4(1), 1970, p. 12.
30  Wilhelm Reich, 'The Impulsive Character Part III', *Journal of Orgonomy* 5(1), 1971, p. 10.
31  Reich, *The Function of the Orgasm*, p. 85.
32  Turner, *Adventures in the Orgasmatron*, p. 74.
33  Reich, *The Function of the Orgasm*, p. 5.
34  Turner, *Adventures in the Orgasmatron*, pp. 82–3.
35  Sigmund Freud, 'The Future of an Illusion', *Standard Edition, Volume XXI*, p. 7.
36  Freud, 'The Future of an Illusion', p.7.
37  Freud, 'The Future of an Illusion', p. 7.
38  Freud, 'The Future of an Illusion', p. 7.
39  For a discussion of Freud's relation to Nietzsche, see McMahon, *Happiness*, p. 441.
40  Sigmund Freud, 'Fixation to Traumas – The Unconscious', *The*

*Standard Edition of the Complete Psychological Works of Sigmund Freud, Volume XVI, 1916–1917* (London: Vintage, 2001), p. 285.

41  Higgins and Chester, eds, *Reich Speaks of Freud*, p. 44

42  Sissela Bok, *Exploring Happiness: From Aristotle to Brain Science* (New Haven: Yale University Press, 2010), p. 132.

43  Freud, 'Civilization and Its Discontents', Editor's Introduction, p. 60.

44  Higgins and Chester, eds, *Reich Speaks of Freud*, p. 44.

45  Higgins and Chester, eds, *Reich Speaks of Freud*, p. 44.

46  Freud, 'Civilization and Its Discontents', p. 76.

47  Freud, 'Civilization and Its Discontents', p. 76.

48  Freud, 'Civilization and Its Discontents', p. 76.

49  Freud, 'Civilization and Its Discontents', p. 77.

50  Freud, 'Civilization and Its Discontents', p. 68.

51  Sigmund Freud, 'Psychotherapy of Hysteria', *The Standard Edition of the Complete Psychological Works of Sigmund Freud, Volume II, 1893–1895* (London: Vintage, 2001), p. 305.

52  Rieff, *The Triumph of the Therapeutic*, p. 30.

53  Reich, *Listen, Little Man!*, p. 111.

54  Wilhelm Reich, *The Mass Psychology of Fascism* (New York: Farrar, Strauss and Giroux, 1933/1970), p. xv.

55  Mildred Edie Brady, 'The Strange Case of Wilhelm Reich', *The New Republic*, 26 May 1947.

56  Turner, *Adventures in the Orgasmatron*, p. 150.

57  Turner, *Adventures in the Orgasmatron*, p. 178.

58  Rieff, *The Triumph of the Therapeutic*, p. 130.

59  Turner, *Adventures in the Orgasmatron*, p. 190.

60  Brady, 'The Strange Case of Wilhelm Reich'.

61  Myron, *Fury on Earth*, pp. 362–3.

62  Myron, *Fury on Earth*, p. 364

63  Mildred Edie Brady, 'The New Cult of Sex and Anarchy', *Harper's*, April 1947, p. 313.

64  Brady, 'The New Cult of Sex and Anarchy', p. 314.

65  Brady, 'The New Cult of Sex and Anarchy', p. 315.

66  Norman Mailer, *Advertisements for Myself* (Cambridge, MA: Harvard University Press, 1992), p. 356.

67  Mailer, *Advertisements for Myself*, p. 338.
68  Mailer, *Advertisements for Myself*, p. 339.
69  Mailer, *Advertisements for Myself*, p. 346.
70  Mailer, *Advertisements for Myself*, p. 346.
71  Mailer, *Advertisements for Myself*, p. 347.
72  Walter Truett Anderson, *The Upstart Spring: Esalen and the Human Potential Movement: The First Twenty* Years (Lincoln, NE: iUniverse, 1983/2004), p. 18.
73  Kripal, *Esalen*, p. 36.
74  Kripal, *Esalen*, p. 39.
75  Anderson, *The Upstart Spring*, p. 19.
76  Anderson, *The Upstart Spring*, p. 54.
77  Kripal, *Esalen*, p. 85.
78  Suzanne Snider, 'est, Werner Erhard, and the Corporatization of Self-Help', *The Believer*, May 2003.
79  Turner, *Adventures in the Orgasmatron*, p. 127.
80  Turner, *Adventures in the Orgasmatron*, p. 128.
81  Turner, *Adventures in the Orgasmatron*, p. 437.
82  Turner, *Adventures in the Orgasmatron*, p. 438.
83  Kripal, *Esalen*, p. 163.
84  Kripal, *Esalen*, p. 163.
85  Turner, *Adventures in the Orgasmatron*, pp. 438–9.
86  According to two unnamed therapists, as cited by Lears, *Fables of Abundance*.
87  Eva Illouz, *Saving the Modern Soul: Therapy, Emotions, and the Culture of Self-Help* (Berkeley: University of California Press, 2008), p. 157.
88  Christina Hoff Sommers and Sally Satel, *One Nation Under Therapy: How the Helping Culture Is Eroding Self-Reliance* (New York: St Martin's Press, 2005).
89  Illouz, *Saving the Modern Soul*, p. 159.

### Chapter 2  Compulsory Narcissism

1  Sheila Heti, *How Should a Person Be?* (London: Vintage, 2014), p. 2.

2  Tom Wolfe, 'The "Me" Decade and the Third Great Awakening', *New York*, 23 August 1976.

3  Elizabeth Lunbeck, *The Americanization of Narcissism* (Cambridge, MA: Harvard University Press, 2014), p. 83.

4  Sigmund Freud, 'On Narcissism: An Introduction', *The Standard Edition of the Complete Psychological Works of Sigmund Freud, Volume XIV, 1914–1916* (London: Vintage, 2001), p. 90.

5  Rieff, *The Triumph of the Therapeutic*, p. 26.

6  Steven Pressman, *Outrageous Betrayal: The Dark Journey of Werner Erhard from est to Exile* (New York: St Martin's Press, 1993), p. 14.

7  Pressman, *Outrageous Betrayal*, p. 15.

8  Pressman, *Outrageous Betrayal*, p. 16.

9  Pressman, *Outrageous Betrayal*, p. 37.

10  Pressman, *Outrageous Betrayal*, p. 38.

11  Pressman, *Outrageous Betrayal*, p. 76.

12  Pressman, *Outrageous Betrayal*, p. 70.

13  Pressman, *Outrageous Betrayal*, p. 71.

14  Pressman, *Outrageous Betrayal*, p. 73.

15  Wolfe, 'The "Me" Decade and the Third Great Awakening'.

16  Pressman, *Outrageous Betrayal*, p. 77.

17  Pressman, *Outrageous Betrayal*, p. 64.

18  Pressman, *Outrageous Betrayal*, p. 77.

19  Peter Marin, 'The New Narcissism', *Harper's*, October 1975, p. 46.

20  Reich, *Listen, Little Man!*, p. 16.

21  Pressman, *Outrageous Betrayal*, p. 70.

22  Pressman, *Outrageous Betrayal*, p. 18.

23  Pressman, *Outrageous Betrayal*, p. 73.

24  Pressman, *Outrageous Betrayal*, p. 71.

25  Nicole Aschoff, *The New Prophets of Capital* (London: Verso, 2015), p. 85.

26  Napoleon Hill, *Think and Grow Rich* (New York: Aristeus Books, 1936/2014), p. 22.

27  Philip Mirowski, *Never Let a Serious Crisis Go to Waste* (London: Verso, 2013), p. 102.

28  Christopher Lasch, *The Culture of Narcissism: American Life in an*

*Age of Diminished Expectations* (New York: W.W. Norton, 1979), p. 85.

29  Ivor Southwood, *Non-Stop Inertia* (Alresford, Hants.: Zero Books, 2011).

30  Lynne Friedli and Robert Stearn, 'Positive Affect as Coercive Strategy', *Critical Medical Humanities* 41(1), 2015, pp. 40–7.

31  Michel Foucault, *The History of Sexuality: The Will to Knowledge* (New York: Penguin Books, 1977), p. 60.

32  Emily Gould, 'Exposed', *New York Times Magazine*, 25 May 2008.

33  Byung-Chul Han, *The Transparency Society* (Stanford: Stanford University Press, 2015).

34  Gould, 'Exposed'.

35  Foucault, *The History of Sexuality*, p. 61.

## Chapter 3  Happiness Inc.

1  Charles Bukowski, *Factotum* (Boston: Black Sparrow Press, 1975), p. 7.

2  Tony Hsieh, *Delivering Happiness: A Path to Profits, Passion and Purposes* (New York: Grand Central Publishing, 2010; unpaginated eBook).

3  Peter Waldman, 'Motivate or Alienate? Firms Hire Gurus to Change Their "Cultures"', *Wall Street Journal*, 24 July 1987.

4  Frank Rose, 'A New Age for Business?', *Fortune*, 8 October 1990.

5  Rose, 'A New Age for Business?'

6  Rose, 'A New Age for Business?'

7  Gurnek Bains with Kylie Bains, *Meaning Inc.* (London: Profile Books, 2007), p. 129.

8  Rose, 'A New Age for Business?'

9  Snider, 'est, Werner Erhard, and the Corporatization of Self-Help'.

10  Landmark Forum, website: http://www.landmarkworldwide.com/the-landmark-forum.

11  Susannah Butter, 'Spiritual Capitalism? Global Fitness Brand lululemon Comes to London', *Evening Standard*, 2 April 2014.

12  Gideon Kunda, *Engineering Culture: Control and Commitment in a High-Tech Corporation* (Philadelphia: Temple University Press, 1992), p. 11.

13  Peter Fleming *Authenticity and the Cultural Politics of Work: New Forms of Informal Control* (Oxford: Oxford University Press, 2009).

14  David Gelles, 'At Zappos, Pushing Shoes and a Vision', *New York Times*, 17 July 2015.

15  Hsieh, *Delivering Happiness.*

16  Letter of 12 August 1986: http://www.lettersofnote.com/2012/10/people-simply-empty-out.html.

17  Jay Stevens, *Storming Heaven: LSD and the American Dream* (New York: Grove Press), p. 110.

18  Oliver Harris, ed., *The Letters of William S. Burroughs, 1945–1959* (London: Penguin, 1993), p. 51.

19  Raoul Vaneigem, *The Revolution of Everyday Life* (Oakland, CA: PM Books, 1967/2012), p. 40.

20  Luc Boltanski and Ève Chiapello, *The New Spirit of Capitalism* (London: Verso, 2005).

21  Joe Kelly, 'Make Conflict Work for You', *Harvard Business Review*, July–August 1970, p. 103.

22  Samuel Culbert and James M. Elden, 'An Anatomy of Activism for Executives', *Harvard Business Review*, November–December 1970, p. 132.

23  Andrew Ross, *Nice Work If You Can Get It: Life and Labor in Precarious Times* (New York: New York University Press, 2010).

24  Guy Standing, *The Precariat: The New Dangerous Class* (London: Bloomsbury, 2011), p. 1.

25  Standing, *The Precariat*, p. 23.

26  Jonathan Crary, *24/7: Capitalism and the Ends of Sleep* (London: Verso, 2013).

27  Rob Lucas, 'Dreaming in Code', *New Left Review* 62, 2010, pp. 125–32.

28  Byung-Chul Han, *The Burnout Society* (Stanford: Stanford University Press, 2015), p. 30.

29  Han, *The Burnout Society*, p. 31.

30  Bertrand Russell, *The Conquest of Happiness* (London: Routledge, 1930/2006), p. 146.
31  Russell, *The Conquest of Happiness*, p. 147.
32  Miya Tokomitsu, *Do What You Love: And Other Lies About Success and Happiness* (New York: Regan Arts, 2015), p. 6.
33  Myerscough, 'Short Cuts'.
34  Tokomitsu, *Do What You Love*, p. 148.
35  Tokomitsu, *Do What You Love*, p. 75.
36  Han, *The Burnout Society*.
37  Juliet Schor, 'Work Less, Live More', *Yes*, 2 September 2011.
38  Jodi Kantor and David Streitfeld, 'Inside Amazon: Wrestling Big Ideas in a Bruising Company', *New York Times*, 15 August 2015.
39  Kantor and Streitfeld, 'Inside Amazon'.
40  Kantor and Streitfeld, 'Inside Amazon'.
41  Franco 'Bifo' Berardi, *Heroes: Mass Murder and Suicide* (London: Verso, 2015; Kindle edn), loc. 336.
42  Kantor and Streitfeld 'Inside Amazon'.
43  Berardi, *Heroes*, loc. 2142.

## Chapter 4  Getting High on Happiness

1  YouTube, 'Leonard Cohen Talks Happiness and LSD in 1966 Animated Interview': https://www.youtube.com/watch?v=Qo WCxK760l0.
2  Kripal, *Esalen*, p. 251.
3  Kripal, *Esalen*, p. 251.
4  Kripal, *Esalen*, p. 319.
5  Anderson, *Upstart Spring*, p. 72.
6  Kripal, *Esalen*, p. 116.
7  Aldous Huxley, *The Doors of Perception* (New York: Harper and Row, 1954), p. 53.
8  Carl Elliott, *Better Than Well: American Medicine Meets the American Dream* (New York: W.W. Norton, 2003), p. 45.
9  Anderson, *Upstart Spring*, p. 57.

10  Alan Watts, *The Joyous Cosmology: Adventures in the Chemistry of Consciousness* (Novato: New World Library, 1962/2013), p. 7.

11  Watts, *The Joyous Cosmology*, p. 17.

12  Watts, *The Joyous Cosmology*, p. 21.

13  Watts, *The Joyous Cosmology*, p. xiv.

14  Watts, *The Joyous Cosmology*, p. x.

15  Timothy Leary, *The Politics of Psychopharmacology* (Berkeley: Ronin Publishing Inc., 2002), p. 17.

16  Anderson, *Upstart Spring*, p. 75.

17  Adam Smith, *The Powers of Mind* (New York: Random House, 1975), p. 43.

18  Smith, *The Powers of Mind*, p. 45.

19  Thomas Szasz, *Coercion as Cure: A Critical History of Psychiatry* (London: Routledge, 2009), pp. 211–12.

20  Leary, *Politics of Psychopharmacology*, p. 13.

21  Thomas Szasz, *Pharmacracy: Medicine and Politics in America* (Westport, CT: Praeger Publishing, 2001), p. xxiii.

22  Norman Dain, 'Critics and Dissenters: Reflections on "Anti-Psychiatry" in the United States', *Journal of the History of the Behavioral Sciences* 25(1), 1989, pp. 3–25.

23  Thomas Szasz, *The Myth of Mental Illness: Foundations of a Theory of Personal Conduct* (New York: Harper & Row, 1961).

24  Szasz, *Pharmacracy*, p. 77.

25  Joost A.M. Meerlo, *The Rape of the Mind: The Psychology of Thought Control, Menticide, and Brainwashing* (Eastford, CT: Martino Fine Books, 2015), p. 35.

26  Meerlo, *The Rape of the Mind*, p. 353.

27  Meerloo, *The Rape of the Mind*, p. 43.

28  Meerloo, *The Rape of the Mind*, p. 46.

29  Meerlo, *The Rape of the Mind*, p. 43.

30  Ken Kesey, *One Flew Over the Cuckoo's Nest* (New York: Viking Press, 1962), p. 34.

31  Peter Kramer, *Listening to Prozac: The Landmark Book About Antidepressants and the Remaking of the Self* (New York: Penguin Books, 1993), p. 4.

32  Kramer, *Listening to Prozac*, pp. 7–8.

33  Kramer, *Listening to Prozac*, p. 18.
34  Kramer, *Listening to Prozac*, p. 10.
35  Kramer, *Listening to Prozac*, p. 19.
36  Kramer, *Listening to Prozac*, p. 20.
37  Elliott, *Better Than Well*, p. 39.
38  Elliott, *Better Than Well*, pp. 43–4.
39  David A. Karp, *Is It Me or My Meds? Living with Antidepressants* (Cambridge, MA: Harvard University Press, 2007), p. 113.
40  Gary Greenberg, *The Book of Woe: The DSM and the Unmaking of Psychiatry* (London: Scribe, 2013), p. 15.
41  Richard P. Bentall, 'A Proposal to Classify Happiness as a Psychiatric Disorder', *Journal of Medical Ethics* 18, 1991, p. 94.
42  Bentall, 'A Proposal to Classify Happiness as a Psychiatric Disorder', p. 97.
43  Greenberg, *The Book of Woe*, p. 19.
44  Greenberg, *The Book of Woe*, pp. 35–6.
45  Carl Elliott, *White Coat, Black Hat: Adventures on the Dark Side of Medicine* (Boston: Beacon, 2010), p. 30.
46  Ivan Illich, *Medical Nemesis: The Expropriation of Health* (New York: Pantheon, 1975), p. 24.
47  Elliott, *Better Than Well*, pp. xv–xvi.
48  Sebastián Serrano, 'Taking the "Smart Drug" Modafinil Made Me Love Work but Hate People', *Vice*, 7 October 2015.
49  Lizette Borreli, '1 in 7 College Students Abuse "Smart Drugs" to Improve Concentration', *Medical Daily*, 14 November 2013.
50  Andrew Leonard, 'How LSD Microdosing Became the Hot New Business Trip', *Rolling Stone*, 20 November 2015.

### Chapter 5  Pleasuring Men

1  'Happy Talk: Simon Critchley + Philip Seymour Hoffman', Rubin Museum of Art, 17 December 2012: http://rubinmuseum.org/media center/happy-talk-simon-critchley-philip-seymour-hoffman.
2  Ray Sanchez, 'Coroner: Philip Seymour Hoffman Died of Acute Mixed Drug Intoxication', *CNN*, 28 February 2014.

3   Epicurus, *The Art of Happiness* (New York: Penguin Classics, 2012), p, 216.

4   Epicurus, *The Art of Happiness*, p. viii.

5   Epicurus, *The Art of Happiness*, p. 325.

6   Epicurus, *The Art of Happiness*, p. 327.

7   Epicurus, *The Art of Happiness,* p. 324.

8   Michel Houellebecq, *Platform* (London: Vintage, 2003), p. 256.

9   Roger Burrows, 'Virtual Culture, Urban Social Polarisation and Social Science Fiction', in Brian D. Loader, ed., *The Governance of Cyberspace* (London: Routledge, 1997), pp. 38–45.

10  Michel Houellebecq, *Whatever* (London: Serpent's Tail, 1994), p. 99.

11  Michel Houellebecq, *Atomised* (London: Vintage, 2001), p. 73.

12  Houellebecq, *Atomised*, p. 73.

13  Houellebecq, *Atomised*, p. 13.

14  Houellebecq, *Atomised*, p. 164.

15  Freud, 'Civilization and Its Discontents', p. 69.

16  Houellebecq, *Atomised*, p. 127.

17  Houellebecq, *Atomised*, p. 154.

18  Houellebecq, *Atomised*, p. 118.

19  Houellebecq, *Atomised*, p. 191.

20  Houellebecq, *Atomised*, p. 70.

21  Wesley Morris, 'Weinstein, Hefner and the Poor Excuse That Explains a Lot', *New York Times*, 27 October 2017.

22  Matt Schudel, 'Hugh Hefner, Visionary Editor Who Founded Playboy Magazine, Dies at 91', *Washington Post*, 27 September 2017.

23  Ross Douthat, 'Speaking Ill of Hugh Hefner', *New York Times*, 30 September 2017.

24  Frank Bruni, 'La Dolce Donald Trump', *New York Times*, 18 July 2015.

25  Elizabeth Lunbeck, 'The Allure of Trump's Narcissism', *Los Angeles Review of Books*, 1 August 2017.

26  Turner, *Adventures in the Orgasmatron*, p. 83.

27  Turner, *Adventures in the Orgasmatron*, p. 437.

28  As quoted in Turner, *Adventures in the Orgasmatron*, p. 437.

## Conclusion: Happiness After Trump

1  Naomi Klein, *No Is Not Enough: Defeating the New Shock Politics* (London: Allen Lane, 2017), p. 48.

2  Glenn Plaskin, 'Playboy Interview: Donald Trump', *Playboy*, March 1990.

3  Amy Sherman, 'Did Donald Trump Inherit $100 Million?', *PolitiFact*, 7 March 2016.

4  James Truslow Adams, *The Epic of America* (New York: Little, Brown, and Co., 1931), p. 404.

5  Norman Vincent Peale, *The Power of Positive Thinking* (New York: Fireside, 1952/2003), p. 45.

6  Peale, *The Power of Positive Thinking*, p. 99.

7  Peale, *The Power of Positive Thinking*, p. 10.

8  See Carl Cederström, 'No Deal, Noel Edmonds. Positive Thinking Can't Cure Cancer', *Guardian*, 8 June 2016.

9  Penelope Schofield, David Ball, Jennifer G. Smith, Ron Borland, Peter O'Brien, Sidney Davis, Ian Olver, Gail Ryan, and David Joseph M.D., 'Optimism and Survival in Lung Carcinoma Patients', *Cancer* 100(6), 2004, pp. 1276–82.

10  Klein, *No Is Not Enough*, p. 48.

11  Diski, *The Sixties*, p. 61.

12  Laurie Penny, *Bitch Doctrine: Essays for Dissenting Adults* (London: Bloomsbury, 2017; Kindle edn), loc. 126.

13  Judith Butler, *Precarious Life: The Power of Mourning and Violence* (London: Verso Books, 2004), p. 20.

14  Aldous Huxley, 'Cynthia', in *Limbo: Six Stories and a Play* (London: Chatto & Windus, 1950), p. 247.

15  Lynne Segal, *Radical Happiness: Moments of Collective Joy* (London: Verso Books, 2017; Kindle edn), loc. 51.

16  Penny, *Bitch Doctrine*, loc. 23.

# Acknowledgements

Although entirely reworked, this book is partly based on some of my previously published essays. In the introduction I have drawn on my essay 'Dangers of Happiness', published in the *New York Times* (18 July 2015). In chapter 1 and 2, I have partly drawn on my essay 'Hundra år av narcissism' ('One Hundred Years of Narcissism'), published in the Swedish magazine *Arena* (3 December 2015). For chapter 2, I've used sections of my essay 'Beware Inspirational Online Images – They May be More Insidious Than You Think,' published in the *Guardian* (10 July 2015); and for chapter 3, I've used passages from 'The 9-to-5 Workday as Liberation', published in *The Atlantic* (10 September 2015).

I would like to thank my publisher Pascal Porcheron for patiently helping me bring this book together. Thanks also to Peter Fleming, Mikael Holmqvist, Jenny Jägerfeld, Michael Marinetto, Darin M. McMahon, Roland Paulsen, André Spicer, and one anonymous reviewer for reading the manuscript and giving me valuable comments. Thanks also to Justin Dyer for excellent editing. Finally, thanks to Sally, Esther, and Ellen – for everything.